The Philadelphia Inquirer

Crisis on the Coast

The risky development
of America's shores

By Gilbert M. Gaul
and Anthony R. Wood

ISBN 1-58822-001-X

Table of Contents

Introduction

====

For more than a decade, reporters Gilbert M. Gaul and Anthony R. Wood discussed working together on a series about coastal development. They shared a fascination with the Ash Wednesday Storm of March 1962, and how development pressures since then had reshaped the nation's shores from modest hamlets to exclusive resorts. Gaul had once been a lifeguard at the Jersey Shore and Wood had worked at an all-night diner at the beach.

In April 1998, the reporters set out to examine the history and impact of the Ash Wednesday Storm. It soon became clear that the storm had served as an unlikely yet pivotal event in the development of the coast. Instead of retreating to higher ground afterward, as might be expected, investors and speculators had flocked there looking for bargains, driving up land values. Developers built back bigger, more expensive homes closer to harm's way. Some of the same towns that had lost hundreds of homes and suffered millions in damage now resembled small cities— with urban densities.

That pattern of building back against the tide has been repeated again and again, with government's help, the reporters found, endangering hundreds of billions in coastal investments.

To document this costly phenomenon, the reporters visited archives around the nation to reconstruct the Ash Wednesday Storm and the origins of federal subsidies benefiting wealthy shore resorts.

They visited virtually every coastal state, interviewing hundreds of builders, homeowners, federal, state and local officials, and weather and climate experts. Using laptop computers, the reporters built a database of property values and storm damage town by town. More than 50 Freedom of Information Act requests produced tens of thousands of federal records detailing disaster aid payments, subsidized loans, flood insurance claims and environmental spending. From these records, the reporters were able to trace and analyze federal spending patterns dating back a half-century.

They also accompanied emergency management officials during on-site inspections following Hurricanes Georges, Bonnie, Floyd and Frances. More than 500 interviews were conducted.

— Philadelphia, March 2000

Part 1

Along the water, disasters waiting for their moment.

The Great Ash Wednesday Storm

Thirty-eight years ago, the most devastating coastal storm in New Jersey history inundated Long Beach Island, drowning seven people, uprooting 600 houses, and tearing the slender barrier island into six pieces.

Along the Eastern Seaboard, from North Carolina to New York, the great Ash Wednesday Storm of 1962 killed 22 people, pounded 50,000 houses, and left $1.3 billion in damage.

So shocking was the destruction that state and federal officials suggested the unthinkable: restoring the vulnerable shoreline to its natural state — a buffer zone off-limits to risky development.

But no one listened.

Aided by generous disaster dollars, federal loans, and a grab bag of other taxpayer subsidies, beach towns built back bigger and closer than ever before.

Instead of a natural buffer, a barricade of pricey real estate now lines the nation's endangered coasts.

Today, Long Beach Island is crowded from dune to bay with vacation homes and investment properties worth nearly $5 billion. It is one piece of a building boom that has transformed the nation's shoreline from seaside hamlets to exclusive resorts worth an estimated $2 trillion.

The unchecked development of America's fragile coasts in the last half-century, a frenzy of building with little national forethought, has come at a hefty price.

The American dream of a house at the beach has turned into a taxpayer nightmare: billions of federal dollars to repair resorts damaged again and again. Billions

$34.3
billion

Jersey Shore Property Values

$8.7
billion

The value of property along the Jersey Shore has skyrocketed by 292 percent since 1962. Adjusted for inflation.

1962   1997

SOURCE: State and county tax records

more to monitor and fix environmental problems — water pollution, unchecked runoff, leaky sewers, vanishing wetlands. And still billions more in decades to come in an endless struggle to guard beachfront real estate from rising seas and inevitable storms.

"These are not random acts of God," said Gregory E. van der Vink, who teaches a course on disasters at Princeton University. "It's only when people build in dangerous places that it becomes a natural disaster."

To accommodate this risky development, the government has been forced into odd and costly roles: The nation's disaster agency sells flood insurance. The Army pumps sand on beaches. Through such policies, Washington lawmakers have painted themselves and the nation's taxpayers into an increasingly costly corner.

In New Jersey, where $34 billion of property lines the eroding coast from Sea Bright to Cape May Point, some state officials concede that efforts to control building have failed. "We had sprawl, sprawl, sprawl all over the place. There was no planning, really," said Judy Jengo, deputy commissioner of the Department of Environmental Protection.

To defend all this investment, state and local officials have erected a Maginot Line of seawalls, groins, jetties, sandbags and underwater reefs extending the entire 109 miles of developed coast. It is the state's counterattack against erosion and the natural migration of barrier islands. Before development took hold, these vulnerable sandbars were reshaped and re-formed by storms and rising seas, without economic consequence.

New Jersey also is home to the nation's most expensive beachfill, a $1.5 billion federally funded project — and officials in New Jersey and other states are lobbying for billions more for other shore projects.

Despite these costly and extraordinary efforts, taxpayer-funded disaster spending in coastal states is increasing dramatically. In the 1990s alone, more than $9 billion in federal disaster aid went to coastal areas, along with billions more in taxpayer-subsidized loans, flood payments and other assistance.

Often, the beneficiaries are seasonal vacation resorts where storms and flooding are as common as snow in Buffalo. Yet under the government's generous rules, man-made disasters are treated the same as natural disasters such as Hurricane Floyd that devastate inland towns where people live and work year-round.

Even modest storms can unleash a flood tide of taxpayer relief. The government has committed billions for roads, utilities, water systems, business loans, landscaping, ball fields, golf courses, marinas and Christmas decorations. It also picks up part of the bill when coastal resorts are forced to evacuate — whether a storm hits or not.

More than ever, the densely developed U.S. coastline stands at risk from rising sea levels, eroding beaches, and a growing number of destructive hurricanes and coastal storms.

For as busy as the 1999 hurricane season was, it did not produce the cataclysmic storm that weather experts say is all but inevitable. A major hurricane striking Miami or New Orleans would cost upward of $100 billion, with taxpayers shouldering much of the cost.

In this book, The Inquirer examines how government policies have encouraged and subsidized hazardous development at the coast, insulating resorts from the consequences of their risky building, and exposing the U.S. Treasury to huge losses for decades to come.

Item: An unparalleled building boom has placed billions in coastal property in harm's way.

Florida is especially vulnerable, with more than a half-trillion dollars of property and a population that has increased fivefold since 1950 — adding 4,000 people a week. All of this building occurred in one of the quietest hurricane periods in history. Florida has not suffered a catastrophic Category 5 hurricane in 64 years. ✳

"We've got a policy in the state that says we won't encourage development in hazardous areas," says Ralph Cantral, director of Florida's coastal management program. "There's obviously a problem with the nomenclature, because most of the coast of Florida is a hazard."

Item: The United States has spent $140 billion on all forms of disaster assistance since 1950. Disaster spending by the Federal Emergency Management Agency alone has jumped 72-fold since the 1950s, adjusted for inflation. One hurricane, Georges in 1998, has cost taxpayers $2 billion. In the previous four decades, only one hurricane cost $500

✳ In 2003 Hurricane Andrew, August 1992 was upgraded to a Category 5 hurricane.

million. Often, aid goes for cosmetic repairs, from street signs to tennis courts.

Item: The government's grab bag of subsidies has fostered an entitlement mentality among many beachfront investors, who often want the government off their backs — except when disaster strikes. The National Flood Insurance Program subsidizes the riskiest beachfront properties. Yet Congress has stopped the program from charging the owners of those properties a fair premium or building adequate reserves, relying instead on the U.S. Treasury.

Item: Investors building along vulnerable coastlines benefit from generous tax breaks. Heading the list: property-tax and mortgage-interest deductions for vacation homes. Owners of rental properties may deduct up to $25,000 in business expenses, from painting to landscaping to utility bills. And if they drive to the beach to check on their property, that's deductible, too.

By comparison, families paying college tuition bills or raising chronically ill children are allowed only modest deductions, with strict income limits. And if you drive to visit a prospective college, sorry, no deduction.

Item: These subsidies help prop up towns dominated by vacation homes, not towns where people live and work year-round. Many beach towns in New Jersey are empty eight months of the year, ghost towns that turn off the traffic lights after Labor Day.

In some towns, the already-tiny year-round populations are being driven out by soaring land values and larger and more lavish resorts. This trend toward upscale building is transforming the character and landscape of the coast from Nantucket to Key West to Seattle, pricing out middle-class Americans.

Competing interests

Many coastal-management agencies, issuing thousands of building permits, are virtually powerless to stop risky building and overdevelopment. That's because land-use decisions are made locally, and that authority is jealously guarded.

"I can tell you without a doubt that several developments we approved make no sense whatsoever," said Courtney Hackney, a member of North Carolina's Coastal Resources Commission, a rule-making body.

North Carolina and New Jersey have issued tens of thousands of coastal building permits since the mid-1970s, yet still cannot say how many beachfront houses line their shores, let alone the effect of all that building. "It would be something that would be useful to know," said Jengo of the Environmental Protection Department.

Regulators struggling to manage coastal development are hamstrung by weak and contradictory rules, legal decisions favoring property owners, and a nearly total breakdown in oversight. The federal Coastal Zone Management program, for example, has spent $1.2 billion since 1972 to help states, yet officials who run it say they have no data to measure its effect.

Today, many coastal programs are stalled in a regulatory gridlock of competing interests among local politicians, developers, environmentalists and state bureaucrats.

South Carolina adopted strict controls on beachfront building in 1988. A developer sued, contending that the rules prevented him from selling two lots on Isle of Palms, a resort near Charleston. The U.S. Supreme Court agreed, and the state had to pay the developer $1.6 million for the lots. The regulators then sold the same lots to builders to recoup their costs — in effect becoming developers.

A loophole in New Jersey's coastal management act allowed thousands of beach houses to be built without permits. In 1993, legislators narrowed the loophole, which had allowed developments of 24 or fewer units to escape scrutiny. However, they added a loophole: exempting storm-damaged houses from review if owners rebuilt.

That year, legislators ordered the Department of Environmental Protection to adopt stricter controls over coastal development. Seven years later, the agency introduced its rules, which were immediately attacked both by builders and environmentalists.

Jengo said rules eventually should do a better job of checking growth along the back bays. As for the barrier islands? It's too late. "They're already built out," she said.

New Jersey has a policy that it will not force property owners to move back as its beaches erode. "It's too late to retreat," says James Mancini, mayor of Long Beach Township for 35 years, and a former developer. "It's a pipe dream of these pseudo-environmentalists."

The coast has been built out, and is too valuable an investment to abandon. The government is stuck. Policies that helped spur development now serve to protect it.

To retreat, or rebuild?

The 1962 Ash Wednesday Storm was a defining moment in the history of coastal development. The nation had a unique opportunity to pull back from the dangerous shoreline. But instead of retreating, beach towns rebuilt. Ironically, storms offered a form of urban renewal, a pattern that was repeated with Hurricane Frederic in 1979; Hugo in 1989; Andrew in 1992; Opal in 1995; and Georges in 1998.

"The building and construction industry loves it," said Miles Lawrence, a 33-year veteran of the National Hurricane Center in Miami. "Let the hurricane tear it up. We'll rebuild it."

On Long Beach Island, the Ash Wednesday Storm did kill the real estate market — for all of three months.

"We wondered how we would sell another house on the island," recalled Herbert Shapiro, one of the island's pioneer developers. But by June of that year, speculators and prospective homeowners returned, looking for bargains.

Today, Long Beach Island is one of the country's most densely developed barrier islands, with shoulder-to-shoulder beach crowds and weekend traffic jams. Most of the $5 billion worth of property is owned by out-of-towners, many of whom were not around for the Ash Wednesday nor'easter.

One who was there was Joe Veitch, a 27-year-old first aid volunteer in 1962. On the morning of March 7, he watched as surging waves severed the island, trapping and drowning two elderly couples. "If we ever got another one like that, I don't think this island could take it," he said.

In the tightly packed village of Harvey Cedars, where the ocean poured into the bay in four places, the front line of 112 beach houses alone is now worth $59 million. That's more than the value of the entire town in 1962, adjusted for inflation.

In 1962, 18-mile Long Beach Island had $136 million of resort property. Today, the 1,064 houses lining the beach alone are worth $566 million. Long Beach Township had property worth $335 million in 1962; today, it's worth $2.2 billion. That's a gain of $944,000 a week for the last 38 years.

"These are just getting to be numbers anymore," says

Janet Ford, who works in the Long Beach Township tax office. "It's not real."

Rising land values have made the Beach Haven bungalow owned by Joe Sprague, who has lived on Long Beach Island most of his 98 years, an endangered species — and also quite an investment.

Sprague bought his cottage a half-century ago for $350. Today, if a buyer were to erect a house on the land, the property would be worth at least $400,000 — a 1,143-fold increase.

Stunning recoveries

Like Long Beach Island, Sea Isle City was decimated by the Ash Wednesday Storm. It took out 30 blocks of beachfront homes and 10 percent of the tax base.

Like Long Beach Island, Sea Isle recovered. And then some.

In 1999, the town's assessed value was $1 billion — 42 times as much as in 1962.

The whine of circular saws and pounding hammers fills the air as the island reshapes itself from modest beach town to increasingly pricey resort.

"Sea Isle is hot," boasts Mayor Leonard Desiderio. "Sea Isle is on a roll."

That's a refrain heard again and again traveling the nation's fragile shoreline, as the equivalent of an economic trifecta — a surging economy, a robust stock market, and a tide of disposable income — combine to fuel an extraordinary building boom.

It is a remarkable, if uncharted, shift that takes many forms:

Nags Head, N.C.: In a town hammered by Tropical

Storm Dennis in August 1999, Malcolm Fearing, a developer, talks about a new generation of cottage. "I had one cottage that I rented for $600 a week. We tore it down and are building a new house with 5,200 square [foot] space, nine bedrooms, and we will rent it for $5,500 to $6,000 a week." He whistles for emphasis. "I don't know why they call it a cottage. It's a damn motel. It's just a pure, doggone investment."

Wrightsville Beach, N.C.: Real estate in the once-quaint family retreat there is worth $1.4 billion, more than double its value only eight years ago. "Wrightsville used to be a working-class beach town; people actually lived there," said North Carolina's Hackney. "Now [houses in] developments cost $500,000 to $1 million and nobody can afford to live there."

Folly Beach, S.C.: Property owners say Hurricane Hugo was the best thing that ever happened to the slender barrier island. The 1989 hurricane tore apart old homes and freed up disaster aid, sparking an economic rally. Says town building inspector Tom Hall: "Now it's almost impossible to find a vacant beachfront lot."

Destin, Fla.: Property values are rising so quickly that city employees cannot afford to live there anymore. Only a decade ago, Destin was a fishing village best known for pompano, mackerel, and the cobia run in the spring. Now, millionaire investors jet into a local airport and stay in gated villas. "Here, there are no architectural guidelines," says Robert P. Franke, the city's planner. "You have Federalist, Mediterranean and Cracker. ... The state's mandate to cut back on sprawl, it's not taking hold here."

In Florida, coastal towns have to submit land-use plans to the state, but they are not models of restraint, said Cantral, the state coastal management director. Were all the planned development to occur, the coastal population would swell tenfold — to 90 million people, Cantral said.

Some resort towns now are as densely built as the nation's largest cities. Census data show that Wildwood is more densely developed than Baltimore; Margate than Newark; Surf City than Camden.

Houses are getting bigger, gobbling up more square feet than ever before and rising higher into the air. In many shore towns, it is nearly impossible to see the ocean, beach or bay because of the walls of buildings.

"Ocean City used to be a family resort," said Tom Cleary, who has lived on a modest rancher on Mariana Lane for 22 years. "People could come down here and buy a small home."

Now, developers are tearing down those homes and putting up duplexes, he said. Now, it's noisier and more crowded. Cars jam the streets. There's no place to park.

"Basically, it ceases to be a family town," he said. "It becomes a greed town. It's strictly greed, greed, greed."

Building bigger

One of the first things Dave Owens did when he went to work for North Carolina as a coastal regulator 20 years ago was take a ride on the beach. Owens, a lawyer and planner, was assigned to sort out development plans for the Currituck Outer Banks, then one of the country's most coveted stretches of virgin barrier island.

For more than a century, the unspoiled stretch of wild dunes, maritime forest and salt marshes had dodged development pressures that had overwhelmed such nearby towns as Kitty Hawk, Kill Devil Hills, and Nags Head. As recently as 1980, only a hundred or so people lived on the 23-mile barrier strip.

Owens faced a unique challenge: How to preserve the distinctive character of the Currituck Banks without closing the door on development for the cash-starved rural county that extends across the shallow sound.

On the makeshift beach road from Virginia to the Dare County border, Owens recalls, "I could drive at 30 m.p.h. and count every house."

Today, there are more than 2,500 houses on the Currituck Banks, 83 times the number two decades ago. Almost all are rental properties and second homes, some worth millions. The barrier island accounts for 62 percent — or more than $1 billion — of Dare County's tax base, but less than 5 percent of its full-time population. At 65 cents per $100 of assessed value, the county has one of the country's lower tax rates.

In summer, the population swells to 30,000 from 500 — even though developers, under pressure from environmentalists and state regulators, agreed to scale back densities. And Route 12, a winding, two-lane blacktop, can barely contain all the Range Rovers, Volvos and minivans carrying vacationers from a half-dozen states.

The county projects that by 2020 the number of houses on the Currituck Banks will more than double, to 6,000. The summer population is projected to swell to 70,000.

Developments such as Pine Island, an old hunting club on an isolated strip of wild dunes, now offer massive oceanfront houses that sleep up to five families and rent for $12,000 a week. Catalogs tout them as perfect for wedding receptions and corporate meetings.

"It used to be people would put a cottage down on the beach, even a nice one," said Currituck County Tax Assessor Tracy Sample. "Now they put down a mansion costing $1 million. It's crazy."

With land prices soaring, owners feel compelled to build bigger to justify their investments, especially if it's a rental property. And, says Bill Hollan, a Pine Island developer, "Part of it is just keeping up with the Joneses."

For planners, the boom has created a new wave of pressures. Route 12 is choked with traffic, as are rural highways carrying vacationers from the Virginia line to the Outer Banks' Wright Memorial Bridge.

In August 1998, when the county ordered an evacuation for Hurricane Bonnie, it took vacationers five hours to drive 12 miles from the county line to the bridge. "People were getting frustrated and driving on the shoulder. People were throwing rocks at them," says Jack Simoneau, the county planning director.

Rapid development may also be outstripping the area's water supply, a thin lens of freshwater that sits atop a lake of saltwater. Some private wells in the older Whalehead Division already have run dry or have suffered saltwater intrusion. The county plans to spend millions to build a desalinization plant, similar to one in the nearby Nags Head area.

Norris Austin, a lifelong resident, watches the breakneck development with a sense of irony. "They come from New York, New Jersey, and they say they like the remoteness of the area," he says. "But then they want to put a 7-Eleven on every corner."

Growing battle-weary

As development has exploded up and down North Carolina's barrier islands, from Currituck to Calabash, so has the toll of storm damage. In August, Tropical Storm

Dennis tore up Hatteras Island, Nags Head, and other towns on the Outer Banks, undermining or destroying scores of houses and causing millions in losses.

Two weeks later, Hurricane Floyd damaged 600 homes on Emerald Isle, where property values had more than doubled in a decade. It took out 100 beach homes worth $27 million on Oak Island. And it exposed septic tanks and the stench of raw sewage at Holden Beach.

For battle-weary officials of North Topsail Beach, Floyd was yet another reminder of their vulnerability. The barrier island is a veritable punching bag for hurricanes, and is viewed by some as a national symbol of the futile fight against nature.

In 1996, it was slammed by Hurricanes Bertha and Fran, which washed away half the town's dunes, eroded 50 feet of shoreline, rendered 350 beachfront lots unbuild-able, and erased $72 million of the resort's tax base.

More than $6 million in federal disaster aid poured in to rebuild dunes, roads, sewers, and damaged public build-ings. The town spent $127,000 planting beach grass in an effort to reestablish its building line.

Two years later, Hurricane Bonnie washed away half of the rebuilt dune and beach grass. Last summer, Floyd fin-ished the job. The storm surge overwhelmed the remain-ing dunes, cut channels across the island, sent waves crashing into condominiums, toppled mobile homes, and crumpled foundations of beachfront properties.

For town officials, the timing could not have been worse. That August they had informed owners of 30 ocean-front properties that they could rebuild on lots taken by the earlier storms. "Now they're probably unbuildable again," said Town Manager Charles A. Hammond.

In a Sisyphean effort, the town is rebuilding its dunes,

and looking to the federal government for financial help. The locals vigorously defend the effort.

"This is a great place," said Scott Murray, a developer in North Topsail. "We just had a little setback."

Reliable data lacking

The coastal economy is vital to the national interest, an engine driving the greatest expansion in U.S. history, accounting for upward of one-third of the gross domestic product.

For years, lobbyists, developers and resort officials have made such claims to buttress their case for billions in federal and state subsidies.

One problem: Even those who make them acknowledge that such assertions are imprecise at best and probably misleading.

"We simply don't have any hard data on the coastal economy," said Charles A. Bookman, a government consultant who helped gather some of the numbers. "Anyone with half a brain can say the coast is a big generator, but what we lack is any kind of analysis."

Most of these claims are based on a sweeping government definition of the coastal economy that stretches from the ocean all the way inland to some of the nation's largest cities.

Under the definition, Philadelphia is a beach town. So, too, the nation's capital. Throw in Wall Street. The Sears Tower. Fanueil Hall in Boston. All part of the coastal economic engine. Or so the government would have you believe.

The definition dates to 1972, when Congress passed new coastal legislation. The law failed to include precise coastal boundaries. That was left to regulators, and they chose a broad definition based on environmental concerns, not economic reasoning.

"We had to make something up," said a Commerce Department official who was involved in the process. "Calling Philadelphia a coastal community may stretch it a bit."

There is, in fact, a coastal economy. It is largely a real estate and tourism market, with most of the high-wage jobs centered in construction and finance. But the majority of the jobs are in the low-wage service sector, census and IRS data show.

Resort officials contend that tourism dollars are a valuable source of revenue for state and federal coffers. But to date, no one has weighed those gains against the generous tax breaks and other subsidies that have encouraged and sustained coastal building.

Development policies are being made in a factual vacuum, acknowledges Howard Marlowe, the nation's premier lobbyist for beach resorts. "We've got lots of anecdotal information, but there's not enough of a national picture."

One who has tried is James R. Houston of the U.S. Army Corps of Engineers, which is in the business of building back storm-damaged beaches.

Houston wrote a widely quoted paper for the engineering magazine Shore and Beach in 1995. It has since become a coastal manifesto.

"Few in America realize that beaches are a key driver of America's economy," Houston wrote. He added that beach tourism contributed $170 billion annually to the economy.

Houston is a physicist by training and one of the

nation's leading coastal engineers. But by his own admission he is no John Maynard Keynes.

"Everything I have is circumstantial," he said. Economic analysis, he added, is something he pursues "on nights and weekends. ... But I think the case is pretty strong."

Among Houston's sources: the World Almanac, USA Today, National Geographic, the Wall Street Journal.

"Some of Jim's stuff is not reliable," Marlowe said.

Nevertheless, Houston's numbers continue to be widely circulated, even by Congress members and regulators.

The year-round populations of many beach towns are declining, not growing, signaling the towns' seasonal nature. Communities such as Stone Harbor and Beach Haven are gaining buildings, not people. Census data show that nearly two of every three shore towns in New Jersey lost population in the last two decades, even though the coastal counties in which they are located were among the fastest-growing areas in the state.

Still, shore officials say tourism is a vital source of jobs. That may be true, but most of the jobs appear to be low-paying — retail clerks, waiters, housekeepers, bartenders.

In 1998, Laurence M. Downes, chairman of the Jersey Shore Partnership, a lobbying group, said tourism accounted for 623,000 jobs statewide with a $13 billion payroll. That works out to an average annual salary of $21,000 — well below the statewide average of $37,500 — and many of the jobs are seasonal.

Nationally, coastal tourism jobs pay a fraction of what other workers earn, an analysis of IRS salary data for 1997 shows. That year, tourism salaries in 16 coastal states ranged from $12,052 in Alabama to $21,874 in New York.

The average U.S. salary for all jobs was $30,336.

On his Web site, Marlowe regularly advertises for economic studies to buttress the case for shore-protection money.

"We're operating on faith," he said, "and we're using the numbers we have to bolster the faith that we have."

Coastal development gone awry: Three snapshots of ruin

PACIFICA, Calif. — In February 1998, Jane Tollini hosted an El Nino party for 40. "The only requirements were that guests wear a flotation device or say a prayer for me," she recalled.

The prayers went unanswered.

Not long after the party, Tollini's cliffside house tumbled over the edge — and most of her life's savings went with it.

"For 10 years, I lusted after that house," said Tollini, the penguin keeper at the San Francisco Zoo.

When she bought it for $250,000 in 1992, there was still 35 feet between Tollini's dream house and the Pacific Ocean.

One morning, Tollini looked out her bathroom window, and part of the cliff had disappeared.

The 1998 El Nino had arrived.

In that string of storms, million-dollar homes were ripped off perches from Malibu to Pacifica, near San Francisco. More than $250 million in federal disaster relief poured into the area.

Nowhere was the damage more dramatic than along Esplanade Drive in Pacifica, a narrow street dotted with California-style bungalows and a view to die for.

Seven of the dozen houses straddling the 65-foot cliff were badly undermined by waves and runoff. One morning, a local geologist advised Tollini to leave. Tollini hesitated. But then a section of porch skidded down the cliff. "It snapped like a cookie," she said.

"I feel great sympathy for what they are going through," said the geologist, Ken Lajoie. "There are no natural hazards, only hazards that are created when we put houses where they aren't supposed to be."

After the 1998 storms, the federal government spent more than $1 million on new seawalls in Pacifica, including one at the base of Esplanade. Another $1 million was used to purchase damaged properties, including Tollini's lot for $98,000.

"The owners got lucky," said Dave Carmany, Pacifica's city manager. "The feds don't cover your bets in Las Vegas when you gamble and lose."

On Lake Erie, no longer enjoying the view

NORTH EAST TOWNSHIP, Pa. — Scientists say the coastline along Lake Erie has risen nearly half a foot in the last 40 years — slowly released from the clinch of a mile-thick glacier that once covered much of northwestern Pennsylvania.

But you would be hard-pressed to tell that standing on the bluffs overlooking the wide blue lake. Huge layers of silty mountainside have crashed down the eroding banks, collecting at the lake's edge. The long pull of waves propelled across the lake on strong southwest currents has gouged the beach and dragged the sand offshore. Undermined trees have collapsed at a sharp angle to the water. And here and there, skeletal remains can still be seen where houses landed among the fissures.

Owners of the modest summer cottages and fancier year-round residences huddled along the wooded shoreline have defended their properties with all manner of devices — huge culvert pipes filled with concrete, ragged stone walls and groins, boulders and concrete slabs, wooden planks, logs, abandoned refrigerators.

"It looks a little like Normandy beach," says Shamus Malone, a staffer with the Department of Environmental Protection, which regulates development along Pennsylvania's 50-mile stretch of Lake Erie.

The average person does not think of Lake Erie as a dynamic coastline. But it is, Malone points out. "People want to get as close as they can for the view, and that creates problems," he says.

Malone has advised more than 1,000 homeowners how to protect their properties, has encouraged others to pull back from the bluff, and has watched houses tumble over. But still the development pressures mount. Billboards for expensive new subdivisions are being erected. State regulations require the homes be set back 50 to 100 feet, depending on the erosion rate. But a home that is safe today could be imperiled in a decade or two, depending on lake levels, storms, and runoff from nearby developments.

"The erosion continues. It will always continue," Malone says. "One year will be especially wet and lake levels will be up, resulting in bigger, more powerful waves. The next, it may be dry and lake levels go down."

The lake is subject to a "dishpan effect" during storms in which water shifts from one end to the other. When the waves crash against the bottom of the sloping shoreline, the energy thrusts upward and slams against the bluff, carving channels and ruts, intensifying erosion.

"That's not a problem so long as houses aren't sitting

too close," said Paul Knuth, a retired Edinboro University professor who has studied Lake Erie erosion. "The problem is created when people move there to enjoy the dynamics of the coast but don't want to live with the consequences or the responsibilities. It seems like the more money people have, the more foolish they are."

Development along the Great Lakes has boomed in the last few decades, with significant erosion and loss of homes reported in Michigan and Ohio. Now, a new wave of problems may loom, as new subdivisions fence in homes already crowding the shoreline, leaving them no place to retreat. "That's what we are going to be facing," says Malone, "homes with no opportunity to move back."

In the Florida Keys, an unwelcome watchdog

BIG PINE KEY, Fla. — Bill Kruczynski is a marked man in the Florida Keys.

Strangers shout at him when he drives his van down U.S. Route 1. Property owners hurry outside if the mild-mannered scientist pauses in their neighborhood. And burly locals have been known to accost Kruczynski in the hardware store, demanding to know why he is ruining the Keys.

Kruczynski's crime: He wants to clean up the polluted water along this fabled necklace of islands stretching south of Miami to the Dry Tortugas. In the Keys, where government is a dirty word and locals take great pride in their independent lifestyle, cleaning up the water is not a simple matter. Many resent the federal government telling them what to do. Last year, a countywide referendum on protecting water quality was voted down. Politicians pointed to the tropical swirl of waters and asked: What problem?

But beneath the sparkling surface of the Florida Keys, there is trouble in paradise. For more than a decade, scientists and government officials have warned residents that water quality in the Keys is seriously taxed by development pressures, poor planning and reckless behavior. Unless things quickly change, they said, the Keys could end up like many other parts of South Florida — gridlocked and polluted.

Many of the lagoons carved by developers in the 1950s and '60s are now stagnant or dead. Studies have found human fecal contamination and viruses leaking from sewers into canals in near-shore waters. Sea grasses, coral reefs and conches are vanishing. Beaches have been closed because of pollution. And Key West's crumbling sewer system has been spewing untreated sewage into the ocean.

Most of these problems can be traced to the popularity of the Keys as a vacation destination. Each year, more than three million people elbow their way down the Overseas Highway, a single, two-lane road, to snorkel, swim, and savor the Keys.

At its peak, population swells to 130,000. Another 30,000 arrive by boat and anchor in the protected harbors.

"It's like we're an opera house that seats 1,000, and we've got one million people who want to come in," said Diane Bair, a Monroe County planner.

Several years ago, the state limited the number of new building permits that the county could issue to 255 a year. Now, the U.S. Army Corps of Engineers is studying how much development the fragile islands can safely support.

To Richard Grosso, an environmental lawyer, the caps come too late. "The Keys are already overdeveloped and have been for many years."

Most of the Keys rely on porous septic systems, smaller treatment plants, and illegal cesspits that flush untreated waste right into the water.

"It's 18th-century technology that we have to bring into the 21st century, Kruczynski said.

Some locals fear Congress plans to clamp down on all development in the Keys. Others, such as Steve Spellman, who has a home along one of the most polluted lagoons in Big Pine Key, say it is about time the feds offered a helping hand.

"The federal government, in its infinite wisdom, ought to come down here and do something," Spellman shouted across the fetid canal one day last summer. "This water used to be clear. There used to be tropical fish in here. Now it's disheartening. Look at this, it's just muck."

To buy in Avalon, he sold a stamp

In 1945, tired of paying hotel bills during his vacations in Cape May, George Lippincott began searching for a property of his own at the beach.

In undeveloped Avalon, the Germantown businessman found an isolated lot tucked away in the dunes and surrounded by cedar, oak and cherry trees. It was just what he was looking for — a quiet, natural setting, with a sprawling view of the ocean.

Lippincott raised the $500 for the 1.2-acre lot by selling a single, rare stamp from his collection. "Can you imagine?" marvels his daughter, Sarah Lee Lippincott Jr., 79, who has put the property up for sale.

Were he alive today, her father would have to sell more

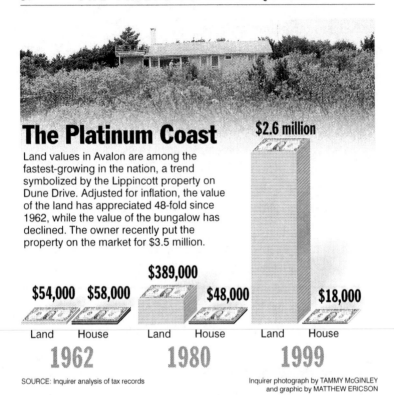

The Platinum Coast

Land values in Avalon are among the fastest-growing in the nation, a trend symbolized by the Lippincott property on Dune Drive. Adjusted for inflation, the value of the land has appreciated 48-fold since 1962, while the value of the bungalow has declined. The owner recently put the property on the market for $3.5 million.

$2.6 million

$389,000

$54,000   **$58,000**   **$48,000**   **$18,000**

Land   House   Land   House   Land   House

1962   **1980**   **1999**

SOURCE: Inquirer analysis of tax records

Inquirer photograph by TAMMY McGINLEY and graphic by MATTHEW ERICSON

than one stamp to buy the lot. He would have to sell his entire collection, his house, and his wholesale lumber business. And he would still have to take out a loan.

The asking price, $3.5 million, is 7,000 times what he paid for the lot. The property has appreciated an average of $1,246 a week — each and every week — for the last 54 years.

What has happened to the Lippincott property is unusual only in that the land has remained in one family's hands for so long; most have turned over several times.

The appreciation is also symbolic of the furious land rush that has reshaped the cultural, economic and environmental character of coastal communities in New Jersey and all along America's shoreline.

"Investing in property in Avalon is like investing in blue-chip stocks," Councilman Chuck Covington has boasted.

That's an understatement. The rise in land values along the 4.2-mile oceanfront has outpaced the booming market. And at an average price of $22,000 per square foot, beachfront property is more valuable than platinum or gold.

At the time of the 1962 Ash Wednesday Storm, the entire Jersey Shore was worth $1.6 billion. Today, Avalon alone is worth $1.7 billion.

George Lippincott had none of this in mind when he bought his lot on Dune Drive in southern Avalon. "Our family and friends said, 'You're nuts! Nobody wants to live in the dunes, for heaven's sake,'" his daughter recalled.

George Lippincott built a modest bungalow with simple lines and a grand view. It had four small bedrooms and one bathroom. There was no electricity on Dune Drive, so he hauled up a line into the dunes.

The family never winterized the cottage and rarely used it in the off-season.

On Oct. 26, 1959, Sarah Lippincott's 39th birthday, her parents transferred the property to her for $1. She made few changes. She installed an air conditioner after her first husband became ill, and, later, a ceiling fan.

Development pushed slowly down the island.

As the number of available lots dwindled, property values in Avalon soared, increasing 16-fold since 1975. Lippincott's property jumped 32-fold, from $79,600, to $2,584,700, records show.

Almost all of that increase was in the land. In 1998, Lippincott's bungalow was assessed at $18,100 — or less than 1 percent of the value of the land. Adjusted for inflation, it has declined in value.

Later that year, Lippincott agreed to sell the property for $3.5 million to Michael W. Rice, president of Utz Quality Foods, one of the nation's biggest makers of potato chips.

The deal is contingent on Rice's winning state and local approval to build a massive new house. Rice already owns one property, on First Avenue, which he bought in August 1997 for $4.6 million, the most ever paid for an Avalon residence.

In an interview, Rice said he was looking for more space. The Lippincott property also offers a better view, he said, "plus some more isolation. It's just a very nice location."

Rice originally proposed building a three-story, 17,000-square-foot house with nine bedrooms, garage, pool, and pretzel-shaped driveway. Builders estimated it could cost up to $7 million. He scaled back his plan after opposition from local property owners and officials.

Sarah Lippincott believes the questions about size and environmental impact are moot, noting that her bungalow is bounded by multimillion-dollar mansions owned by some of Philadelphia's corporate chieftains.

"It's a little late to start worrying about disturbing the naturalness of Avalon," she said. "That battle was lost 25 years ago. That's past. That's gone. Whatever they build on, one more property won't matter anymore."

Temple University Urban Archives

The 1962 Ash Wednesday Storm devestated Harvey Cedars, N.J.

JOHN COSTELLO / Inquirer Staff Photographer

Harvey Cedars today. The 112 beach front houses are worth $59 million.

Part 2

Amid a fury of construction,
a grace of hurricane quiet

Coming soon,
the $100 billion storm

At daybreak, the six hours of hell wrought by the most powerful hurricane ever to hit Miami subsided. The winds had wailed as loudly as the frantic rescue sirens that filled the streets.

Stunned residents and visitors ventured from their houses and hotels to watch the first light of day break upon the devastated landscape. Some knelt to kiss the earth.

Then, suddenly, the gales howled anew, this time up to 150 m.p.h. People who had been lured outside were defenseless against hurtling debris. "The air was streaked with garbage cans, automobile tops, doghouses, furniture," wrote a storm survivor, L.F. Reardon.

The storm would leave 372 people dead, more than 6,000 injured, and $1.6 billion in damage in today's dollars.

It has been more than 73 years since Miami was hit dead-on by a Category 4 hurricane like the one that struck that morning of Sept. 18, 1926. Experts now warn that Miami, having narrowly escaped the worst of Hurricane Andrew in 1992 and Floyd in September, is long overdue for another catastrophic storm.

When it comes, it won't be a $1.6 billion-dollar storm. If that 1926 hurricane were to strike today, the bill would be more than $80 billion, researchers calculate.

In fact, hurricane specialists believe that any year now, the United States will be blindsided by a $100 billion hurricane — one that would rock the insurance industry and sock taxpayers with a staggering repair bill.

Statistically, a hurricane catastrophe is most likely to strike South Florida, where million-dollar high-rises, luxu-

If Past Hurricanes Occurred Today

The chart shows how much damage past hurricanes would have done if they had occurred in 1998, taking into account increases in population and construction.

Storms from the last 25 years are highlighted in gray.
Figures in billions.

Storm	Year	Cost Inflation-adjusted	Cost If storm occurred in 1998		Storm	Year	Cost Inflation-adjusted	Cost If storm occurred in 1998
1 SE Florida	1926	$1.6	$80.6		16 Carla	1961	2.3	7.9
2 Andrew	1992	31.7	36.9		17 Hazel	1954	1.7	7.8
3 Galveston	1900	0.8	29.7		18 NE U.S.	1944	1.1	7.2
4 Galveston	1915	1.4	25.1		19 SE Florida	1945	0.9	7.0
5 SW Florida	1944	1.1	18.8		20 Frederic	1979	4.4	7.0
6 New England	1938	4.3	18.5		21 SE Florida	1949	0.4	6.5
7 SE Florida	1928	0.3	15.4		22 S. Texas	1919	0.3	6.0
8 Betsy	1965	7.6	13.8		23 Alicia	1983	3.1	4.5
9 Donna	1960	2.2	13.4		24 Celia	1970	0.5	3.7
10 Camille	1969	6.2	12.2		25 Dora	1964	0.3	3.5
11 Agnes	1972	7.7	11.9		26 Fran	1996	3.2	3.5
12 Diane	1955	5.0	11.4		27 Opal	1995	3.2	3.3
13 Hugo	1989	8.7	10.5		28 Cleo	1964	0.7	2.7
14 Carol	1954	2.8	10.1		29 Juan	1985	2.2	2.7
15 SE Florida	1947	0.8	9.3		30 Audrey	1957	0.8	2.7

SOURCE: National Oceanic and Atmospheric Administration

ry hotels, and pricey vacation homes line the coast. But it could be almost anywhere along the built-out Gulf and Atlantic Coasts — perhaps New Orleans, or Galveston, Texas.

The threat has little to do with global warming. It has everything to do with human development. A largely unregulated, unplanned building boom has transformed the nation's coasts, placing nearly $2 trillion worth of property in harm's way.

During the last 50 years, this unprecedented period of building has paralleled an era of hurricane quiet.

Now, hurricane experts warn, the party is over. A new era of dangerous land-falling hurricanes is under way, an era that could last until 2020 or longer.

"Our memories are so short," said Jerry Jarrell, who just retired as director of the National Hurricane Center in

Miami. "We say it ain't going to happen again. Well, it's happening again."

For 40 years, William M. Gray of Colorado State University has studied tropical cyclones. And for 16 years, with impressive results, he has been making long-range forecasts of the numbers of hurricanes that will form in the Atlantic and the Gulf.

Everything he sees tells him that the United States has entered a period of costly hurricanes. The kind that pack tornado-level winds and haul walls of water across whole towns. The kind that occurred in 1926, and several times in the '40s and '50s.

A convergence of data and common sense tells Gray, an atmospheric scientist, that nowhere in the country is the potential more frightening than in South Florida.

To illustrate, he points to two maps of hurricane tracks in Florida. The first, sparsely marked, shows storms prior to 1995. "This 25-year period, nothing," he says. "This is the period when people buy homes and develop."

Then he points to the second map, one that looks to be covered with the mad scribblings of a 2-year-old. "Those are the tracks of the '40s and '50s. Now what happens when we go back to this?" he asks.

We're about to find out, Gray believes.

He is holding a terrifying portrait of high hurricane season in Florida. It is a vision of palm trees bent to the ground, of flying wood and metal, of wildly blowing curtains of water and debris, of mobile homes and sailboats tossed like footballs, of ambulances and tent cities and contaminated water.

But at this moment, from his office in the foothills of the Rockies, it is a vision that only this gangling man in the argyle sweater can see.

That vision might seem far-fetched to many people in Florida, which has had an extraordinary run of luck over the last three decades. From 1941 to 1950, 20 land-falling hurricanes hit Florida, six of them major, packing winds from 111 to 150 m.p.h. From 1971 to the present, a mere six hurricanes, only one of them major, made landfall there.

The residents of Fort Lauderdale, Miami, and the Keys have been particularly blessed. Southeastern Florida was assaulted by 11 intense hurricanes from 1900 to 1960, but only one, Andrew, in the last 39 years.

The intense hurricanes are the important ones, causing more than half of all private insured losses nationwide.

Andrew, not the Big One

A decade ago, insurance industry officials estimated that in a worst-case scenario, a hurricane would leave Florida with a $7 billion bill.

They were wrong. And in 1992 they would find out how wrong. At 5:05 a.m. on Aug. 24 that year, Andrew buzz-sawed across South Florida, near Homestead. More than 135,000 houses were damaged or destroyed, and more than 250,000 people were left homeless.

The price tag was staggering: More than $30 billion, including $20 billion in insured losses, the most expensive hurricane on record.

Yet for all the trauma, Andrew was not the Big One. Not even close.

In geographic coverage, Andrew was actually a small storm. The band of maximum winds was only about nine miles wide, roughly the distance from Philadelphia International Airport to City Hall.

In most hurricanes, the storm surge — the wall of

water dragged ashore — does most of the damage. But Andrew moved so quickly that flooding was negligible in South Florida.

More significant, Andrew followed a relatively benign path.

Andrew's track minimized the damage to Dade County, the government said in its post-storm report. Had the eye of the storm crossed the coast just 10 miles north, it would have devastated downtown Miami, probably causing greater loss of life and more than $50 billion in insured losses.

Hurricanes have been churning in the Atlantic Basin and the Gulf of Mexico for thousands of years. Only in modern times have the storms interacted with a combustible additive: human development.

Consider that Florida has added two-thirds of its population — more than 10 million people — since 1950.

One indicator of the change in building levels came courtesy of Hurricane Opal, a Category 3 hurricane that made landfall in the Florida Panhandle in October 1995.

The flood damage was greater than the combined total of damage from all coastal storms in the state in the previous 20 years — $400 million.

Ironically, Opal unleashed a frenzy of speculation, driving up property values. "We started getting calls from 'bottom fishers,'" recalled Ira Mae Hewatt, a Realtor. Prices jumped 20 percent in the first six months after Opal.

Beachfront lots that sold for $250,000 before Opal now garner $400,000 or more. A drive along the 2.5-mile Gulf Boulevard reveals towering condominiums fetching up to $1 million per unit and pricey new resorts with marble porticos and sleek pools — and few empty lots.

"What have we learned after Opal?" asked county administrator Hunter Walker. "I don't think we learned anything."

In 1950, the year the Fort Lauderdale region was leveled by a Category 4 hurricane that produced a record 155-m.p.h. wind, Broward County had a population of 83,933. Today, it is close to 1.5 million. In 1950, Dade County's population was less than 500,000. Today it is more than two million. Fewer than 30,000 people lived in the Keys in 1950. Now, more than 80,000 do.

In the last five decades, the number of seasonal residences has more than quadrupled in Florida, from 78,247 to 360,515, according to state figures. In Collier County, on the southwest coast, the number of seasonal residences has jumped 2,000 percent.

From 1909 to 1965, the Florida Keys took direct or indirect hits from major hurricanes 12 times; Broward County, 10 times; and Collier County, eight.

Yet no major hurricane has affected any of those areas, directly or indirectly, since 1965.

A false sense of security

The majority of the nation's coastal residents have never experienced a major hurricane.

And in virtually every coastal city of any size from Texas to Maine, the United States is building toward a hurricane disaster, the National Oceanic and Atmospheric Administration said last year.

With satellites and radar providing early warning, it is unlikely that the United States will suffer a disaster such as Hurricane Mitch, blamed for more than 12,000 deaths in Central America in 1998, or the great Galveston hurricane of 1900 that killed 8,000 people.

But though hurricane monitoring has improved immeasurably in the last 25 years, Gray believes that fancy satellite and radar graphics have given people a false sense of security.

"People see stuff on television, and they think great advancements are being made," he said, "but the actual track prediction is only a little bit better."

Hurricane specialists believe that under the wrong circumstances, significant casualties are possible along the developed coasts.

Emergency-management officials worry that coastal areas have become so crowded that evacuation routes, such as those linking the Florida Keys, North Carolina's Outer Banks, and New Jersey's barrier islands to the mainland can't handle all the evacuees.

In September, as Hurricane Floyd menaced the Southeast coast, gridlock quickly followed evacuation orders, from Florida to South Carolina. Floyd was able to move a lot faster than most of the traffic. It was the nation's largest peacetime evacuation.

Jarrell, the retired National Hurricane Center director, says he is concerned about New Orleans in particular. "It takes forever to evacuate it," he said. "Their fallback is to use the Superdome as a shelter. It may not even be safe, but it's the best you can do. Standing room only is better than dying."

In 1997, a hurricane-evacuation study presented a chilling portrait of what might happen in New Jersey if a major storm approached.

"The clearance times calculated for Cape May County are among the highest calculated in the United States," it said.

"Basically, what it shows is that you can't get the people off the barrier islands," said Clark Gilman, the state's director of floodplain management.

That document, prepared by the U.S. Army Corps of Engineers, the Federal Emergency Management Agency, and the state police, did not create much of a stir. State officials did not circulate the study, Gilman said.

If a hurricane hit Atlantic City, Gilman warned in an earlier report, it could catch people unprepared. Many casino guests, he said, are unfamiliar with their surroundings and unaware of the peril imposed by a coastal storm or hurricane.

Close calls, nothing more

At the north end of Atlantic City, where the Boardwalk confronted the worst of the howling storm winds dead-on, a wall of water submerged Virginia Avenue on Sept. 14, 1944.

The waves were at least 25 feet high. They smashed the world's most famous promenade into dangerous chunks of debris that rode the surging waters and crashed into buildings. Four feet of water swamped an area from Virginia to Maine Avenues, and floodwaters swelled to the tips of the parking meters on Atlantic Avenue.

The bulk of the destruction came from storm waves churned by a cyclone that was agitating the ocean like a massive plunger as it moved from south to north about 30 miles offshore. The storm would kill at least 10 people in New Jersey, erase 60 percent of the Atlantic City Boardwalk, and devastate Sea Isle City, Strathmere, Cape May, and Wildwood.

The damage was stunning, about a quarter of a billion

JOHN COSTELLO / Inquirer Staff Photographer
Shore flooding at Summer Street, Strathmere, N.J, during a February 1998 storm.

dollars up and down the Jersey coast, by state police estimates.

But perhaps the most unusual aspect of the 1944 hurricane is this: Nothing like it has happened since. Hurricane Gloria, in 1985, was a close call, passing 26 miles off the coast. However, it moved swiftly, 44 m.p.h., and it approached at low tide. The '44 storm was traveling 35 m.p.h. and approached at high tide.

Like the rest of the East Coast, the beach towns of New Jersey have enjoyed a remarkable period of hurricane immunity.

"They're big-time due," said James Eberwine, the marine-forecasting specialist with the National Weather Service in Mount Holly.

"When it happens, there's going to be disbelief," said Anthony Gigi, another weather service meteorologist.

A direct hit by even a modest hurricane could be catastrophic, Eberwine said. And a hurricane of the same path and intensity as the 1944 storm would do more damage now, observed Gilman, the state floodplain-management director. Sea level has risen about 8 inches since 1944, the result of melting glaciers. That translates to a more dangerous storm surge.

A storm today would also encounter a far different landscape. Over the last 50 years, the total value of property in New Jersey's coastal towns has jumped fivefold, adjusting for inflation.

A moderate hurricane is a realistic threat to the Shore and the rest of the Northeast coast, especially late in the hurricane season, which ends Nov. 30. Although few hurricanes can survive the cool ocean waters of northerly latitudes, the ones that do are especially erratic and dangerous. The chilly waters do not have time to drain the power from a storm caught in a fast-moving air stream.

"If a hurricane leaves the Gulf Stream at 35 m.p.h., it's like a skater out of control," said Nicholas Coch, a hurricane specialist at Queens College, in New York.

In 1938, a rapidly moving Category 3 hurricane plowed across Long Island, slamming into Connecticut and ravaging the forests of New Hampshire and Vermont. That storm remains the Northeast's worst hurricane. It killed at least 600 people.

On then-sparsely populated Long Island, another area long overdue for a catastrophic storm, it ripped open seven new inlets and killed 50 people.

In the 1930s, 162,000 people lived in Suffolk County, N.Y., which took the brunt of the 1938 hurricane.

Today, two million do.

Gray and his team at Colorado State think they understand the reasons for the long hurricane lull and, alarmingly, why it's over.

Gray relies on old-style statistical relationships, rather than computer models. Two trends are especially ominous: The waters in the North Atlantic have warmed up, and it's raining again in western Africa.

In active hurricane periods, sea-surface temperatures are above average in the North Atlantic, and below average in the South Atlantic. North Atlantic temperatures have been above average for the last five years, and so have the numbers of hurricanes.

The oceans are far slower to change than land masses, and temperature trends can last 25 to 40 years, said Christopher W. Landsea, a hurricane researcher with the National Oceanic and Atmospheric Administration.

It appears that the Atlantic contrasts have a profound effect on the upper atmosphere off the west coast of Africa. That's a spawning region for tropical storms. It is just far enough from the equator, about 300 miles, for a cyclone to pick up spin from the Earth's rotation. And it is a perfect location for a storm to mine deep, warm water.

To get started, a hurricane needs 80-degree waters, penetrating to a depth of 150 feet. To make the most of that heat energy, air currents have to rise several miles into a moistened atmosphere. The air condenses, releasing more heat energy and supplying more power to the storm.

A cool North Atlantic, however, favors dry winds that keep the air from rising and shear off would-be storms.

When the Sahel region of western Africa is dry, hurricanes are infrequent. But the Sahel has just been through its wettest five-year period since the 1960s, Landsea said.

Since 1995, as if on cue, the Atlantic Basin has set a record for the number of named storms for a five-year period.

Gray said that only one thing has saved the United States from catastrophic damage in that period: Dumb luck — luck that, statistically, can't last.

When the luck runs out, the experts say, insurers, property owners and taxpayers will pay a price.

When hurricanes move landward, forecasters are put in the hotseat

MIAMI — When a monster hurricane spirals toward the East Coast, it's a sure bet that a 25,000-square-foot vault, reinforced with enough concrete to pave a mile of I-95, will take a direct hit from a storm of second-guessing.

Satellites have forever changed the way hurricanes are tracked, but it is up to the forecasters here at the National Hurricane Center to figure out where a storm is headed.

They will be the first to tell you that they do not always know. But that will never stop the people who make evacuation decisions from demanding immediate answers.

In the case of Hurricane Floyd in September, the storm's magnitude and hard-to-predict path led to the biggest peacetime evacuation in U.S. history. More than three million people were chased out of a long strip of coast from Florida to South Carolina, only to be trapped in massive traffic jams.

The evacuated area escaped major damage.

Still, Miles Lawrence, a 33-year veteran of the hurricane center, said he had no regrets about the warnings that touched off the evacuations. About the only thing certain in a hurricane, he said, is that some people are going to be evacuated unnecessarily.

Every hurricane packs its own surprises and, as a

storm approaches, the windowless hurricane center can be a window onto the borders of chaos.

The center is a technological bulwark of the government's $4 billion program to upgrade the weather service. It is strung with 50 miles of wiring; with a few keyboard clicks Lawrence can summon state-of-the-art satellite images of the symmetrical fury of an approaching hurricane and the most sophisticated radar that taxpayers can buy.

Yet Lawrence prefers to plot the course of these potentially deadly storms on plain charting paper with colored pencils, a primitive compass, and a plastic ruler. At his elbow he keeps a yellowing road atlas.

The red marks are the positions from an Air Force reconnaissance plane that has flown into the storm. The green are from Doppler radar. The veterans prefer the pencils to the gizmos because it gives them a better feel for a storm, says a colleague, Edward N. Rappaport.

Nevertheless, sometimes it is hard to determine precisely where a hurricane is, let alone where it is going.

In 1998, for example, with landfall only 15 hours away, the satellite and the hurricane-tracking plane had the eye of Hurricane Bonnie at two different points, about 20 miles apart. This is common. The planes are looking straight down, but the satellite is looking from an angle, the so-called parallax, 22,000 miles above the Earth.

Emergency managers and coastal property owners do not really care about the parallax view. They want to know whether they are going to get whacked, and when.

Like Bonnie, which caused more than $300 million in damage in the Carolinas, Floyd was targeting some of the most densely developed areas of the East Coast.

It had traveled more than 1,000 miles, forming off the

west coast of Africa, then gliding across the Atlantic along the weak east-to-west airstream of a large weather system centered near Bermuda — the Bermuda high.

Floyd grew into a monster, fueling itself on warm tropical waters, exploding with the heat of convection, and expanding into one of the largest hurricanes on record.

Once it neared the coast, it would be lifted north by a front moving across the mainland United States.

Or so the models said.

But on Monday, Sept. 12, Floyd and its 155-m.p.h. winds kept bearing down on Florida, making a dangerously close approach.

Ordinarily, Lawrence views his work with a sense of detachment.

But he took Floyd quite personally. He lives in Miami. "I get excited when it's my hometown," he said.

On that Monday, it looked as if Floyd might make a house call at the Lawrence residence. "It was so big we thought it could punch through this front," said Stephen Leatherman, director of the International Hurricane Center, which is affiliated with the Miami center. That's why Florida was evacuated, he said.

At almost the last minute, the storm made a sharp turn north, as predicted, paralleling the shoreline and lashing the east coast of Florida with rains and high winds. As it churned northward, state officials in Georgia and South Carolina ordered evacuations.

A weakened Floyd finally made landfall near the Carolinas' border, where it mutated into a monumental rainstorm, causing hundreds of millions of dollars in flood damage. Coastal areas to the south avoided catastrophic damage.

Lawrence said the hurricane center had no choice but

to put up the warnings, even though they led to the great, chaotic exodus.

"Maybe the average citizen or the average leader would rather take the risk," he said.

Nor'easters administer a perpetual threat

Though a hurricane is a real threat at the Jersey Shore in any given year, it is a remote one. By contrast, a nor'easter — a winter coastal storm — is all but a certainty.

"Hurricanes are terrible, but they don't happen very often," said Robert Dolan, a leading expert on coastal storms. "I think there's a much higher probability of a nor'easter raising hell and havoc along the Atlantic Coast."

The Shore is hit by nor'easters every year. Every two years, a coastal storm causes significant damage.

In fact, the most damaging storm to hit the Shore since it became a popular playground was a powerful nor'easter that struck in March 1962, causing $500 million in damage.

The most damaging recent storm battered the coast in December 1992, causing $265 million in insured losses and releasing $57 million in federal aid.

If a 1962-level storm hit today, it could make a mockery of hundreds of millions of dollars in shore-protection expenditures and endanger the biggest beachfill project in the nation's history, now under way in North Jersey. Because of a rise in sea level, the waves would be at least 10 percent higher.

A dangerous combination of higher seas, chronic erosion, and swollen back bays will make future storms much more damaging, meteorologists and geologists warn.

The region from Long Beach Island to Cape May Point

is especially vulnerable, and areas that face due northeast — such as the inlets at the north ends of Avalon and Atlantic City — are all but taunting nature.

Nor'easters get their names from the sometimes ferocious winds they generate from the northeast. Because winds circulate counterclockwise around a storm's center, the Shore confronts winds from the east and northeast as the storm tracks up the coast. Unlike hurricanes, winter storms can cover an immense area.

Often, the strongest winds at the Shore occur when a storm is off Cape Hatteras, N.C., a common breeding area. The clash of polar air invading southward and warm air over the Gulf Stream supplies the raw material to set a storm in motion.

The big storms are incited by the jet stream, the west-to-east wind that is the upper boundary between cold and warm air. When the jet is powerful, it acts like wind lifting smoke from a chimney.

The waves fomented by the winds cause the bulk of a nor'easter's destruction — even more than storm surge, the water level above the normal tidal height.

The ferocity of a storm is difficult to quantify, but Dolan and Robert Davis, an associate at the University of Virginia, have devised their own 1-to-5 rating scale, akin to the Saffir-Simpson scale for rating hurricanes. The 1962 storm was a 5; a February 1998 nor'easter that hit the Jersey Shore, a 1.

The December 1992 storm ranked a 5, and was the strongest since 1962. Wave heights approached 30 feet, and storm winds persisted for 140 hours, figures that had been unmatched since 1962.

For all their havoc, coastal storms are vital to barrier islands, Dolan says. Without them, the sandy strips would simply drown in place under rising sea levels. Though the storms contribute to erosion, they also keep the island above water by piling other sand landward.

For thousands of years, coastal storms occurred without incident. But now buildings are in the way, and the sand displaced landward is considered a nuisance by local officials.

After every big storm, work crews remove it from the streets along with beach debris. Federal taxpayers often pick up most of the bill.

Sand and debris removal is one of the biggest categories of government-subsidized disaster aid.

The Shooting Gallery:
Hurricane paths, decade by decade

The development boom that has transformed the nation's coasts from seaside hamlets to exclusive resorts has taken place during a quiet hurricane period. Yet damages from the period's few storms have reached unprecedented levels. A return to a period of even normal hurricane activity would result in catastrophic losses, experts predict.

The maps show the paths and number of hurricanes that have hit the United States during each decade since 1940.

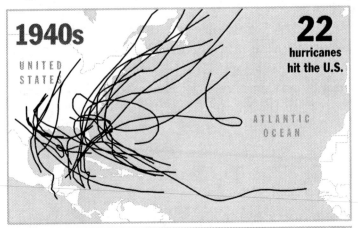

1940s

UNITED STATES

ATLANTIC OCEAN

22 hurricanes hit the U.S.

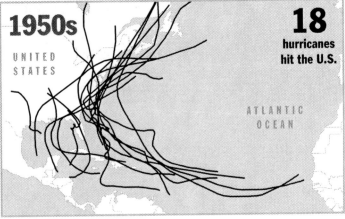

1950s

UNITED STATES

ATLANTIC OCEAN

18 hurricanes hit the U.S.

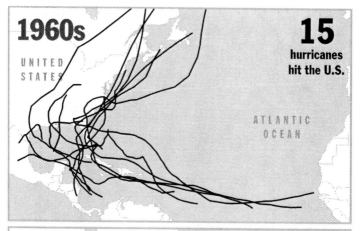

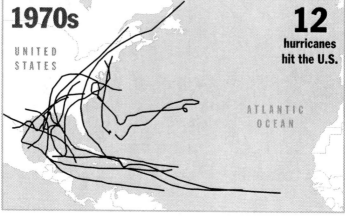

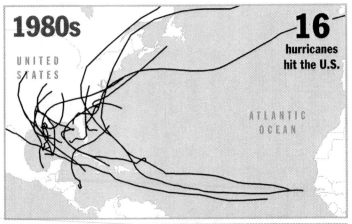

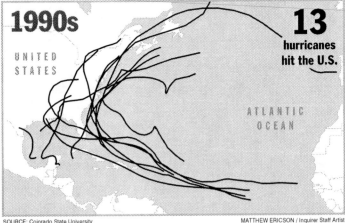

MATTHEW ERICSON / Inquirer Staff Artist

Part 3

Uncle Sam, insurer of the first resort

Exclusive beach towns rely on government dollars to rebuild

It wasn't much as storms go. There was heavy rain and strong winds, flooding in low-lying areas, and beach erosion. In short, about what you would expect from a winter storm along the New Jersey coast.

But to local officials, Washington bureaucrats and President Clinton in early 1998, this was much bigger than just a storm. It was a federal disaster.

Gov. Whitman pleaded for help, contending that the state and beach resorts did not have the resources to cope. And on March 3, 1998, a month after the storm, the President responded, declaring Shore counties disaster areas, eligible for federal aid.

Taxpayer dollars poured in — nearly $3.3 million. But not for what you might imagine. The U.S. government agreed to repair tennis courts, fix a gazebo, patch boardwalks, replace street signs, pay for landscaping, buy tourism brochures, and rebuild beaches.

And the victims?

Records show that there were no injuries, deaths or destroyed homes. The Federal Emergency Management Agency (FEMA) budgeted more for paperwork and administration than it did for aid to individuals.

"We didn't ask a lot of questions for why we got that disaster [declaration]," said Joe Painting, a state emergency management official.

Nor, apparently, was New Jersey as desperate as federal officials had been led to believe. The state finished the

Disaster as a Growth Industry

The average number of federal disaster declarations has tripled since the 1950s, in part because of loose financial criteria and politics. Spending by federal emergency agencies, after adjusting for inflation, has soared 72-fold, to $24 billion.

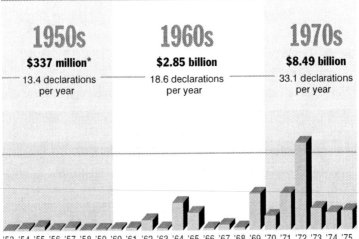

1950s	1960s	1970s
$337 million*	**$2.85 billion**	**$8.49 billion**
13.4 declarations per year	18.6 declarations per year	33.1 declarations per year

'53 '54 '55 '56 '57 '58 '59 '60 '61 '62 '63 '64 '65 '66 '67 '68 '69 '70 '71 '72 '73 '74 '75

SOURCE: FEMA.   * Amount spent from 1953-1959.

year with a $1 billion surplus — enough to give New Jersey property owners rebates averaging $120.

By comparison, it would have cost the state's eight million residents just 41 cents each to have paid for the storm damage themselves.

An aberration?

Hardly.

Thanks to the largesse of Washington, an ever-expanding definition of federal emergencies, and a legacy of risky building along the coast, disasters have become a growth industry. Among the beneficiaries are exclusive beach towns and resorts with some of the lowest tax rates in America.

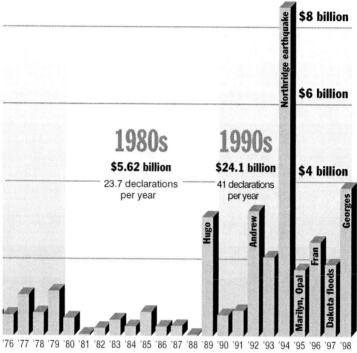

MATTHEW ERICSON / Inquirer Staff Artist

Many use taxpayer-funded disaster relief as a form of insurance for their municipal property. They carry little or no coverage, relying on federal funds to cover storm damage, including ruined Christmas decorations, flooded tennis courts and snapped flagpoles.

The average number of annual federal disaster declarations has more than tripled — from 13.4 in the 1950s to 41 in the 1990s. The number peaked in 1996, an election year, at 74.

Disaster spending by FEMA increased from an inflation-adjusted $337 million in the 1950s to more than $24 billion in the 1990s, a 72-fold spike. Yet there were more frequent and far more powerful hurricanes in the 1950s than in the 1990s.

All told, federal agencies from the Department of Housing and Urban Development to the Small Business Administration have spent an estimated $140 billion on disasters since the 1950s.

And despite promises from Congress and the Clinton administration about closing disaster loopholes, the numbers keep going up.

More than one-third of all disaster declarations — 410 awards — were made from 1990 through 1998. They accounted for a disproportionate share of all federal disaster spending — 58 percent of the nearly $42 billion, inflation-adjusted, handed out by FEMA since 1953.

In 1998, FEMA awarded Delaware nearly $2.9 million for the same coastal storm that hit New Jersey, with almost one of four dollars — $656,000 — for administrative overhead. The rest went to local governments, not individual victims. Gov. Tom Carper contended that the storm posed "a significant threat" to the state's economy. Yet Delaware finished the year with a $432 million surplus.

And in September, Clinton again took out the taxpayer checkbook for the Jersey Shore after Whitman wrote that waves, wind and storm surge from Hurricane Floyd had "caused substantial damage." Her Sept. 17 appeal was made before state emergency officials had completed an assessment. Floyd caused hundreds of millions in damage inland, but barely grazed the coast. The Shore declared eligible for federal aid anyway.

Increasingly, disaster funds are propping up beach towns that have built in harm's way — part of an unprecedented development boom that has transformed the nation's coasts from seaside hamlets to exclusive resorts with property worth $2 trillion. In this scenario, government disaster aid has become a form of entitlement, benefiting relatively wealthy beach resorts yet paid for by all taxpayers.

Now, lax government rules and a surge in risky development are threatening to drive up disaster costs even more. An examination of 10,000 federal disaster records and more than 100 interviews has found:

Loose criteria. By law, state and local governments are supposed to receive federal disaster aid only when it is beyond their financial capability to respond. But there are no objective criteria, and almost anyone can qualify. On average, two of every three requests for help are approved.

Lax financial standards. In 1986, Congress prohibited FEMA to use strict means tests for disaster aid. Nor does the agency consider a town's property values or tax rate. This allows wealthy beach towns like Avalon, N.J., and Westport, Conn., to shift to federal taxpayers some of the risks and costs of doing business in a storm-prone area.

"Disasters should only be declared when it's beyond the capability of municipalities, and this has gotten way out of hand," said Richard W. Krimm, a former top FEMA executive.

An unofficial standard. FEMA has an unofficial standard for awarding aid. To qualify, storm damage is supposed to exceed an amount equal to $1 for each resident of a state. That 15-year-old figure has never been adjusted for inflation. How did the agency come up with $1? "It was a round number," joked Robert J. Adamcik, a FEMA official.

Damage is supposed to exceed $2.50 per capita at the ✶ county level. But FEMA bases its estimates on year-round population figures, which seriously underestimate the size and wealth of summer vacation resorts, making it easier to

✶ 2004 – $2.77 Per Capita

collect disaster aid.

Vulnerable property. In the last decade, FEMA has directed $9 billion in disaster assistance — or two of every five disaster dollars — to vulnerable coastal resorts and U.S. territories, including Puerto Rico. Private insurers' costs also are soaring, with hurricanes responsible for three-fourths of the $43 billion in claims between 1950 and 1992. And Small Business Administration disaster loans, which provide up to $200,000 for housing repairs and $40,000 for contents, also are rising.

Governments take advantage. FEMA has awarded state and local governments nearly $13 billion in the last decade, more than half of all of the agency's disaster payments. Millions have gone for mulch, wood chips, bocce courts, baseball scoreboards, greenhouses, equestrian trails, lifeguard stands, water coolers, swing sets, garbage cans, lawn fertilizer, toys, insurance deductibles, and salaries and food for prisoners who clean up after storms.

Golf course subsidies. In the 1970s, Congress expanded disaster benefits to include public golf courses and marinas. Since then, FEMA has spent more than $10 million on those facilities — and more than $200 million on parks and recreation sites.

After a 1992 nor'easter, the agency approved nearly $3 million in claims to repair the Borough of Atlantic Highlands' municipal marina, and $185,000 to rebuild the Village of Loch Arbor's beach club. The Links at Key Biscayne, a golf course near Miami, claimed $300,000 to replace trees damaged by Hurricane Andrew in 1992.

"Why be prudent in locating a home or business when the government will offset or blunt the losses with all of these subsidies?" asked Raymond J. Burby, a University of New Orleans natural-hazards expert.

Added Gregory E. van der Vink, who teaches a course on disasters at Princeton University: "There is no free-market system that would help create natural selection, with people bearing the consequences of their risky land use. The natural selection is blunted by federal disaster relief and insurance, and it's the wealthiest segment of society that benefits most."

FEMA director James Lee Witt agrees that the nation spends too much on disasters, and says he is trying to cut costs. The agency is pouring hundreds of millions into efforts to make beach towns and other areas "disaster-resistant."

FEMA also has proposed tightening financial eligibility and requiring governments to carry insurance on public buildings. But Witt faces stiff opposition from those who benefit from lax standards. "I'm getting huge, huge political pressure not to publish this [insurance] rule," he said.

New Jersey cashes in

The transformation of routine storms into federal disasters has accelerated under the Clinton administration.

Without stronger standards, FEMA contends that it has little choice but to hand out disaster dollars. Congressional delegations and governors lobby heavily for aid, often appealing directly to the President.

The agency's own loose rules compound the problem. Some FEMA regions are tougher than others when determining eligibility. This has opened the door to the disaster equivalent of grade inflation. In some cases, disasters are declared even before damage is tabulated.

Nearly 60 percent of all declarations are for less than $10 million, records show. Almost 40 percent are for less

The federal government picks up 75 percent of the cost of repairing public property after disasters strike, regardless of the tax rate or wealth of the town. Here are selected examples of what it agreed to pay Jersey Shore towns after a February 1998 nor'easter. The average tax rate in New Jersey at the time was $2.43 per $100 of equalized value.

Town	Tax rate	Project	U.S. Share
Avalon	$0.91	Tennis courts	$1,193
		Stop signs	$1,525
Cape May Point	$0.86	Dune fence	$7,313
North Wildwood	$2.37	Dog signs	$3,106
		Manholes	$23,606
Ocean City	$1.62	Street signs	$1,883
		Sewer cleaning	$2,375
		Playground work	$1,786
Sea Isle City	$1.42	Tourist brochures	$1,831
		Wood chips	$788
Stone Harbor	$1.00	Fishing pier	$2,257

SOURCES: New Jersey Legislative District Data Book, 1998 (tax rate per $100 of equalized value); Federal Emergency Management Agency (projects and federal share).

than $5 million. In some cases, local governments could raise these funds with a minimal tax increase. Yet FEMA rarely takes that into consideration when handing out disaster dollars.

That was the case in federal Disaster Declaration 1206 covering Atlantic, Cape May and Ocean Counties in the winter of 1998.

On Feb. 18, Whitman wrote "with utmost urgency" to request federal aid after heavy surf and flooding hit the coast that month.

"The storm caused extensive damage and has continued to severely tax state, county and local resources left bare from a very hectic storm season," the governor wrote FEMA and Clinton.

Whitman's request did not spell out why the state

could not afford to cover the damage itself, and made no mention of New Jersey's surplus. FEMA, for its part, appears to have accepted the governor at her word. Documents obtained under the Freedom of Information Act provide no evidence of agency officials' testing the state's claims. One record shows that the state even failed FEMA's $1 test.

The agency calculated disaster repairs at $4.7 million for the Shore counties. That worked out to 60 cents for each state resident. "Normally, the way things work . . . you have to have $1 in damages per person," said Painting, the state emergency official. "We got a disaster turned on for less than that."

How did FEMA conclude that New Jersey and the beach resorts could not pay for their own repairs?

That's secret.

FEMA considers its recommendations to the president privileged documents that describe the "deliberative process" of a federal agency. It refused to provide all but the cover sheet of those letters. And those appear to repeat almost verbatim the information supplied to the agency by the state.

FEMA records do show that the coastal storm produced relatively minor damage, primarily to the dunes protecting private beach homes and local roads. Under the category "Impact on Individuals," FEMA officials penciled in "0." In fact, nearly two-thirds of disaster dollars budgeted for Declaration 1206 went to local governments, not individuals.

After a December 1992 coastal storm, Jersey Shore towns requested thousands of dollars from FEMA to replace damaged holiday decorations.

"That storm wiped out all of their Christmas lights. In

most cases, it was paid. It was eligible," Painting said.

Overall, New Jersey received more than $100 million in federal disaster aid in the 1990s, much of it for coastal damage.

Such public-assistance aid accounts for more than half of FEMA's $22 billion in disaster expenditures in the last decade — double what it spends on individuals.

Most of that individual aid is for temporary housing for year-round residents displaced by storms. Though FEMA does not cover vacation properties, owners benefit from taxpayer-funded repairs to sewers, roads, water systems and beaches. Many also qualify for low-interest loans and have federally backed flood insurance.

In effect, the agency functions as a taxpayer-funded charity for coastal towns, states and territories, providing millions in aid regardless of their wealth.

After Hurricane Georges in September 1998, FEMA approved $26,513 in disaster claims to repair pigpens and replace 44 piglets at two prison farms in Puerto Rico. The agency approved $2,160 for aviaries and $200,850 for baseball fields and a billboard. Millions more went to repair roads, utilities, and damaged government buildings.

Such generous subsidies are a disincentive to safe coastal development, in effect rewarding governments that build on barrier islands and other storm-prone sites, concluded a 1993 report by the federal Office of Technology Assessment.

Local officials offer another view. "My personal philosophy is as long as they have these programs available, I'm going to do everything I can to take advantage of them. That's my job," said Dave Carmany, city manager in Pacifica, Calif., which received more than $1 million for El Nino storms in 1998.

Normally, the federal government picks up 75 percent of the cost of public assistance, rarely more. If local governments do not have the cash to meet their share, FEMA will provide a low-interest loan. The agency has handed out more than $171 million to 10 governments, including such storm-prone U.S. territories as Puerto Rico, American Samoa, the Marshall Islands, and the U.S. Virgin Islands.

FEMA also has a loan program to cover economic losses. Nearly half of those loans, $46 million, have been written off by the agency.

One reason FEMA spends so much on public assistance: Many local governments have not insured their public property, or have underinsured, counting on taxpayers to help them rebuild. The agency has proposed that local governments be required to cover at least 80 percent of their property value. But the governments and their congressional representatives are resisting.

Witt said the proposal would be a tough sell; the entire California delegation opposes it, and a congressional study of the cost impact has stalled. "So I mean, what do you do, you know?" Witt said.

Another proposal, calling for minimal financial standards in declarations, is expected to go ahead, with the backing of some key members of Congress. It calls for using the $1 per capita threshold, adjusted for inflation, and would set a $1 million minimum on public-assistance losses.

"I think seriously we're moving in the right direction," Witt said, "but I think it's at a snail's pace in comparison to what it should be."

Few options for FEMA

In 1979, Hurricane Frederic, a bruising Category 3 storm, ripped across Dauphin Island, Ala., leveling 140 homes and causing millions of dollars in damage. Among the casualties was the only bridge linking the private resort to the mainland.

Since then, the barrier island has been struck by four hurricanes and has received millions in federal disaster aid, including $32 million for a new bridge. Hurricane Georges, a relatively weak storm, lashed the island in September 1998, sweeping away 41 houses and leaving dozens of others teetering in the Gulf of Mexico on stilts.

FEMA approved more than $2 million for repairs, including nearly $1 million to build a protective dune in front of private houses on the vulnerable west end of the island. An additional $3.9 million in federally backed flood claims flowed to property owners.

One might think, given Dauphin Island's vulnerable nature, that federal officials would try to prevent more building there.

They can't.

That power lies almost entirely with local officials, who control building and zoning laws. The most FEMA can do is use its disaster dollars to encourage safer building.

Powerless to stop risky building, FEMA attempts to hold down future losses by investing in costly preventive measures. FEMA calls this strategy mitigation. It has become the agency's rallying cry.

Under Witt, whom Clinton named FEMA director in 1993, FEMA has increased funding for prevention and education programs. The agency has begun marketing its message with almost religious zeal, asserting before one

JOHN COSTELLO / Inquirer Staff Photographer

Hurricane Georges in 1998 moved sand across Dauphin Island, Ala., leaving homes in the water.

news conference, "A disaster does not have to be disastrous, and Director Witt will explain why."

Last June, Witt urged mayors to make their communities "disaster-resistant."

"We do not have the technology to prevent disasters," he said, "but we absolutely have the technology to prevent disaster damage."

FEMA has handed out $1.2 billion in mitigation grants in the last decade, and the money is a valuable new subsidy to beach towns looking to armor themselves against nature's fury.

FEMA officials contend that mitigation works, and point to savings — $2 in disaster aid for every $1 spent raising houses, buying storm shutters, repairing sand dunes, and fortifying water and sewer systems.

But those "savings" are dwarfed by soaring disaster costs: $337 million in the 1950s, $2.85 billion in the 1960s,

$8.49 billion in the 1970s; $5.62 billion in the 1980s, and $24.1 billion in the 1990s, adjusted for inflation.

"There really isn't that much FEMA can do, so it is pushing mitigation," said Rutherford H. Platt, a University of Massachusetts natural-disaster expert. "And what happens is, it ends up giving these towns bonuses for doing things they should be doing themselves."

With no means testing, and taxpayers picking up 75 percent of the cost, the mitigation grants are popular politically. Last year, FEMA started attaching Vice President Gore's name to major-grant announcements, on orders from the White House, FEMA said.

In 1997, Witt introduced Project Impact, a highly publicized attempt to showcase disaster prevention in select communities. The program has awarded millions in grants to 200 communities. The towns are selected by state officials and approved by the agency.

The Project Impact communities represent 1 percent of the 19,000 flood-prone communities nationwide. And, though growing, mitigation funds are a fraction of FEMA's budget. The agency spends more on administrative overhead than prevention, documents show.

One recipient of Project Impact funds is hurricane-prone Dauphin Island. It plans to upgrade drainage systems and buy storm shutters for private houses.

In 1979, Frederic submerged most of the 15-mile-long island and caused $7 million in property damage, not including the cost of replacing the bridge.

FEMA officials warned that building a new bridge would encourage development on the barrier island resort — and lead to more disaster spending. The agency was right on both counts.

Development boomed after the bridge was completed

in 1982. A $9 million sewer plant was installed three years later, at taxpayer expense. Today, Dauphin Island is crowded with an estimated $250 million in property, including vacation homes that rent for $1,500 a week and up.

Most of the 41 owners whose houses were destroyed by Georges have decided to rebuild, said Jimmy Reaves, local compliance officer. Ironically, the hurricane seems to have boosted land values. Last year, officials approved a seven-story hotel on the beach.

Dauphin Island has a year-round population of approximately 1,500, which swells tenfold in summer. About 70 percent of properties are second homes and rentals.

"People live here disaster-free for 300 days of the year, and the other 65 can be hell," council member Alma Wagner said. "But as long as they have that 300 days of happiness on the water, they will continue to build bigger and better."

FEMA is helping. The agency has approved nearly $1 million for the temporary dune in front of private houses. The agency says the proposed dune is designed to protect city-owned utilities, not rental properties.

Dauphin Island remains at extreme risk. The west end is flat and has no trees or vegetation, leaving scores of houses exposed to fierce hurricane winds. Storms and erosion have placed the state's construction control line more than 100 feet offshore, under several feet of water.

More than a year after Georges, there was still little beach. Strollers had to duck under houses on the west end and maneuver around stilts.

What beach is left on the west end is largely private. Owners have placed "No Trespassing" signs at the ends of their driveways.

That has not stopped FEMA from helping to advertise

the island. After Georges, the agency approved $1,125 to replace the resort's welcome sign.

Hurricane-prone Puerto Rico dependent on U.S. disaster aid.

CANOVANAS, Puerto Rico — The squatters began arriving here shortly after Hurricane Hugo leveled their wood and tin homes. Nobody knew how many. There were no roads or addresses. And the government didn't keep count.

They erected huts and shacks from whatever scraps they could find. Some were no bigger than closets or boxes. In an act of defiance, they called their shantytowns Hugo 1 and Hugo 2, after the famous 1989 hurricane.

In the capital, San Juan, inspectors looked the other way. They had little choice. By law, houses costing less than $40,000 did not require a building permit. Nor could inspectors fine squatters or evict them from the flood-plain. They were barely surprised when Hurricane Georges gutted the makeshift settlement in September 1998.

"Welcome to the horror," said Henry Contreras, an engineer for the Department of Regulations and Permits, looking out over a sea of blue tarps, covering crumpled shacks.

FEMA paid for the tarps, meant to keep out rain, and doled out disaster checks to the squatters. Some will use the money to fix their shacks. Others will find another place to squat. It will be that way until the next hurricane sweeps across the island, and the cycle is repeated.

Puerto Rico, surrounded by pale blue seas, may be the most hurricane-prone island in the world. It has been

The Puerto Rican Shooting Gallery

Puerto Rico is one of the most hurricane-prone islands in the world. More than $3 billion in federal disaster payments have flowed to the island in the last decade alone.

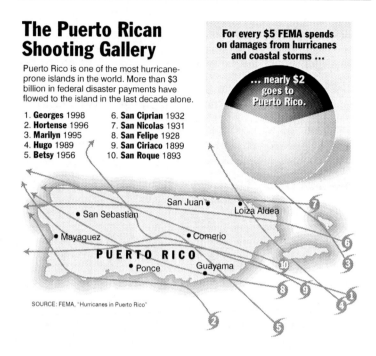

For every $5 FEMA spends on damages from hurricanes and coastal storms ...

... nearly $2 goes to Puerto Rico.

1. **Georges** 1998
2. **Hortense** 1996
3. **Marilyn** 1995
4. **Hugo** 1989
5. **Betsy** 1956
6. **San Ciprian** 1932
7. **San Nicolas** 1931
8. **San Felipe** 1928
9. **San Ciriaco** 1899
10. **San Roque** 1893

PUERTO RICO

San Juan • Loiza Aldea
• San Sebastian
• Mayaguez • Comerio
• Ponce Guayama

SOURCE: FEMA, "Hurricanes in Puerto Rico"

struck by more damaging hurricanes in the last century than anywhere else. It is also highly dependent on U.S. taxpayers to rescue it after storms.

In the last decade alone, FEMA has spent more than $3 billion on disaster payments in Puerto Rico, following hurricanes and coastal storms. That includes $2 billion for Georges, a relatively weak Category 2 hurricane. At least $250 million in other federal subsidies have flowed to the island in Georges' wake.

Think of it as a form of government-sponsored hurricane insurance for island residents, who pay no U.S. taxes.

"It's a hard problem," Contreras said. "The people have no resources and they know they can receive benefits."

What makes this remarkable is that Georges was not the Storm the Century. It wasn't even the storm of the decade. The highest official wind speed recorded by the

National Weather Service in Puerto Rico was 83.6 m.p.h. One station reported a gust of 102.3. By contrast, maximum sustained winds when Hurricane Andrew raked southeast Florida in 1992 were 135 m.p.h. San Felipe, a hurricane that pummeled Puerto Rico in 1928, packed winds of 140 m.p.h.

Still, FEMA officials were stunned by the level of destruction they found after Georges. More than 200,000 homes had been damaged, including an estimated 18,000 that in essence had been destroyed. Nearly 65,000 houses required tarps.

"Things were out of kilter," said Cliff Oliver, a FEMA official who examined the damage. "There shouldn't have been so much damage based on the building code and wind speeds."

One explanation: FEMA discovered that the government was using a 30-year-old building code. The law had gaping loopholes, and there was almost no enforcement. Tens of thousands of homes had been built without permits, many of them shacks in dangerous floodplains and along mountain cliffs prone to landslides. An entire subculture had emerged in which poor people ignored the permitting process, and no one stopped them.

In Canovanas, government officials are not even sure who owns the land. Titles are nonexistent or passed by word of mouth. "This whole area is anarchy," said Manuel Cardona, an administrator with the Department of Regulations and Permits.

"In my opinion, most of the totally destroyed homes were homes that didn't comply with the building code," said Carlos O. Gonzalez-Sanchez, the department's executive director.

"The thing is, since 1945, when the planning board was

created, there has been a construction waiver for poor people," he said. "Now, we are proposing by the year 2001 all construction in Puerto Rico has to have a permit."

Changes in the building code and enforcement also are proposed. "It's not going to happen overnight," Gonzalez-Sanchez said. "It is going to take decades and decades."

And millions in taxpayer aid to build stronger, safer houses. FEMA is helping island officials take steps to cut losses. But even FEMA officials don't think the island can be made disaster-proof. "I don't think so, honestly," said FEMA's director, James Lee Witt.

Puerto Ricans live in a shooting gallery for hurricanes. On average, the island suffers a direct hit once every 7.5 years, and an indirect hit every four years.

An analysis of hurricane data shows that the island is overdue for a catastrophic storm. It has not suffered a direct hit from a Category 4 or 5 hurricane since 1928 — 72 years. Historically, a Category 4 or 5 has hit here every 21 years.

As costly as Georges was, a more powerful hurricane would be catastrophic. "A Category 4 or 5 would be devastating," said Justo Hernandez, a FEMA official. "We were really lucky this time."

Part 4

A flawed program facilitates
building in hazardous areas

A risky business plan

Imagine for a moment you are a fresh graduate of the Wharton School. You want to start an insurance company and are seeking financing.

Your business plan:

Locate in one of the most dangerous areas of the country, the storm-swept coastline.

Pick out the riskiest customers you can find — customers likely to file claims again and again — and then give them a discount.

Agree not to cancel policies, no matter how many claims are filed.

Operate without reserves for covering catastrophic losses — a standard industry requirement — in order to keep rates artificially low.

Who would back such a risky venture? No one in the real world of business.

But the federal government does through taxpayer-backed flood insurance. It covers beach houses and investment properties that flood again and again. It has lost huge sums. The program has no reserves to speak of. And, as an emergency backstop, it relies on the U.S. Treasury, borrowing hundreds of millions to bail it out in tough times.

"Even though we have to pay it back with interest, we're still having to borrow money as a company," said James Lee Witt, director of FEMA, which operates the flood program.

"If you and I were the president and CEO of that company and had to go to the bank to borrow that money, the bank would eventually get tired of loaning you that money," Witt said.

The flood program, which covers 4.1 million properties

nationwide, is different in other ways. It allows private insurance companies to earn commissions for selling federal policies — while incurring no risk. And the government spends millions advertising its insurance, further encouraging development along the vulnerable coast.

In 1968, Congress created the National Flood Insurance Program in an effort to slash disaster costs from floods and curb development in flood-prone areas.

The program's objectives have not been realized, a year-long investigation, including analysis of thousands of flood claims nationwide, has found.

Disaster costs from floods, hurricanes and coastal storms are increasing, not declining. Risky development continues along many beach towns and back bays, with tens of thousands of houses erected in the floodplain each year. And with more property than ever exposed to nature's fury, and no reserves, the flood insurance program faces potentially catastrophic losses — with no one to bail it out except taxpayers.

Among the findings:

Faulty design. Normally, insurance rates are based on risk. The greater the risk, the more you pay. The flood pro-

A Decade of Flood Losses

Seven of the 10 greatest losses under the National Flood Insurance Program since it began in 1978 were caused by coastal storms (highlighted in white).

Flood	Cost
Louisiana flood 1995	$582 million
Hurricane Opal 1995	394 million
Hurricane Hugo 1989	375 million
Nor'easter 1992	341 million
Midwest floods 1993	270 million
Texas flood 1994	216 million
Hurricane Fran 1996	211 million
Eastern U.S. blizzard 1993	210 million
Northeast flood 1996	174 million
Hurricane Andrew 1992	167 million

SOURCE: National Flood Insurance Program

ELIZABETH V. ROBERTSON / Inquirer Suburban Staff
Drain pipes in Ocean City, N.J., carry water from flood-prone areas to the ocean. Ocean City's flood losses are among the nation's highest.

gram gives huge discounts to its riskiest customers —
older, flood-prone properties — while charging newer
properties full rates. Three of every 10 of the National
Flood Insurance Program's properties are still subsidized:
1.2 million properties, resulting in an average annual
shortfall of $450 million on those properties.

Insuring vacation homes. Six of every 10 National Flood
Insurance Program properties are in beach towns, including vacation homes and investment properties on storm-
prone barrier islands. All told, $309 billion in federally
backed coastal property is at risk, including $11 billion in
New Jersey. Coastal areas account for a growing share of
the program's most expensive claims, including seven of
the 10 costliest disasters.

Repeat offenders. Some properties flood again and
again but still receive discount rates. They represent fewer
than 2 percent of all properties with federal flood insurance yet account for nearly one-third of losses — $200 mil-
lion annually. Congress has blocked attempts to impose
surcharges on the owners of these properties or to limit
payouts. Now it wants to use tax dollars to put some of
those houses on stilts, another subsidy.

Paper savings. FEMA contends that the flood program
saves taxpayers $770 million a year in flood damage pay-
ments nationwide through its promotion of safer building
standards. That is damage the agency calculates would
have occurred had builders used older standards. It does
not reflect new flood damage resulting from development
in floodplains that FEMA is powerless to stop.

Deficit financing. FEMA says the flood insurance program is designed to be self-supporting, meaning premiums cover losses. Yet over its 30-year history, the program
has lost at least $1.2 billion, and recently had to borrow

more than $1 billion from the U.S. Treasury just to pay claims. As of last year, it owed taxpayers more than $700 million, with interest. This is like a homeowner who borrows money to balance his checkbook and then claims he is operating in the black. "In essence, we're using our borrowing capacity as our reserve," said Edward T. Pasterick, FEMA's chief financial officer.

No reserves. Congress forbids the flood program to charge enough to cover catastrophic losses, which normally would be funded from reserves. That keeps rates low for the riskiest customers. But it leaves the program vulnerable to large losses. Those losses could top $6 billion in a worst-case event, federal officials say. To build adequate reserves, the government would have to double what it collects now, and more than double what it charges its riskiest policyholders.

"I think the initial intention was to discourage development in hazardous areas," said Raymond J. Burby, a University of New Orleans expert in coastal hazards. "That hasn't occurred. In fact, flood insurance has had the opposite effect. Instead of making it more expensive to build in hazardous areas, it has encouraged and subsidized those risks."

FEMA's Witt acknowledged that the flood program was flawed and said he was taking steps to fix it. He said a $200 million plan to elevate the most frequently flooded properties would cut losses.

"We've got to clean this program up. We've got to change the way we're doing things," Witt said.

If he can do that, Witt added, he will turn the flood program over to private insurers. "It should be part of the private market at some point," he said.

Given the monumental risks along America's crowded,

storm-swept coasts, Witt may have a hard time finding takers.

Private insurers wary

How did the federal government's disaster relief agency become the insurer of last resort for some of the endangered real estate on America's coasts?

Private insurers wanted no part of flood insurance. It was too risky, they said. Unlike other natural disasters, such as earthquakes and tornadoes, floods are predictable, particularly on the coast, where hurricanes and other storms strike year after year. Thus, only those at risk would buy coverage, resulting in certain losses for insurers.

For decades, Congress struggled with the issue. One of the staunchest supporters was Harrison A. Williams Jr., a Democratic senator from New Jersey, who introduced flood bills in 1962, 1963 and 1965. Williams contended that because insurers could not afford to offer private insurance, the responsibility should fall to the government. In 1964, Sen. Claiborne Pell, a Democrat from Rhode Island, privately wrote Williams in support of his effort, noting that Pell's Newport home could be "a great beneficiary of such a bill."

In 1965, lawmakers expressed concern that flood insurance would reward risky coastal development. Williams responded that he was proposing coverage only for safe development — "not for those who build in unsuitable areas. Gracious. I have seen people build homes literally on stilts, out in the Atlantic Ocean."

Some members of Congress proposed including a buffer strip along the ocean where insurance would not be written. The idea was to discourage risky building. When legislation finally passed in 1968, however, it did not include buffers, setbacks or other protections. Congress agreed to cover property regardless of where it was built — including on stilts in the ocean.

Nor did Congress distinguish between investment properties, vacation homes, and year-round residences. A working farm in North Carolina was treated the same as a vacation home on an eroding barrier island.

This provided a boost to coastal developers, who advertised the availability of cheap, taxpayer-backed flood insurance, and helped pave the way for an unprecedented wave of beachfront construction, putting yet more property in harm's way.

Today, an estimated $2 trillion in property straddles the nation's vulnerable shorelines and back bays, much of it second homes built during decades of below-normal storm activity. Federally backed flood insurance covers more than $300 billion of that property. It insures residences for up to $250,000 and contents for $100,000.

Federal officials contend that coastal development would have occurred without government flood insurance. And they say their efforts to elevate houses and promote stronger building codes encourage safer development.

"If you've got somebody who's going to build a $1.5 million home on the ocean, he's going to build it regardless of whether he gets protection," Witt said.

Still, at least 2.3 million buildings have been constructed in the most flood-prone areas of the country — the very areas where the government says it wants to curb risky development. Those properties have suffered at least $1.5 billion in flood damage since 1978, FEMA records show — losses that virtually no private insurer would have risked covering.

The agency is only now undertaking a detailed review of the 30-year-old program. "There have been a lot of judgments about policy made without knowing with any precision what the effects have been," said Gilbert F. White, one of the nation's leading experts on coastal hazards.

Initially, Congress expected private insurers to share the risks with the government. And for a time, they did. But then, after a dispute in the 1970s, FEMA assumed all of the risk.

Later, insurers did share in one aspect of the program — its revenues. In the 1980s, FEMA created the Write Your Own flood insurance program. Private insurers were allowed to sell government flood insurance and earn commissions, now totaling $165 million annually. Today, private companies sell most of the flood insurance nationally for the government. But they do not share the risks. Policyholders and taxpayers are responsible for those.

Witt said he would like to see that changed. "If we can get this to the point that we feel comfortable . . . then it should be privatized," he said.

'An unholy alliance'

Failing to include buffers was not the only flaw in the National Flood Insurance Act of 1968. While Congress touted the legislation as a way to direct safe development along the coasts and rivers, it avoided the most effective tool for limiting hazardous development: land-use controls.

Congress was powerless to tell communities where they could build. As long as towns met the federal flood program's minimal requirements, they were allowed in.

Municipalities could develop their vulnerable shorelines as they chose, earning millions in tax revenues, yet depend on federally backed flood insurance and taxpayer disaster aid to protect them against storms.

Towns and states have adopted widely varying rules. Some, such as North Carolina, have established setbacks for new buildings, while others have not.

"FEMA believes that local government will act as a shining knight," said Rutherford H. Platt, a coastal expert at the University of Massachusetts. "Local government is in an unholy alliance with speculators and banks to develop their tax base, and has a strong interest in promoting shorefront development. It's their economy."

Those pressures were evident in September 1998 after Hurricane Georges destroyed 41 homes on the western end of Dauphin Island, Ala. It was the fifth hurricane to strike the vulnerable barrier island in two decades.

Two days after the storm, Brad Cox stood only feet from the Gulf of Mexico, surrounded by crumpled houses, twisted wood pilings, and concrete slabs where vacation properties recently had perched. His employer, Boardwalk Realty Inc., manages rental properties that were now perilously close to the water.

"I'm really concerned what you will say about these houses, as close as they are to the water now," Cox told Ron Nybakken, a FEMA official assessing the damage. "You could condemn them or order them moved. I'm really concerned."

Cox needn't have worried. Flood program officials lack the power to condemn houses or order them moved. Those are local decisions. The most the agency can do is require an owner to elevate if rebuilding — and only then if inspectors find that damage has reduced the property's market value by 50 percent.

"Quite frankly, some of those decisions are controversial," said Todd Davison, a FEMA executive in Atlanta, "but FEMA has no authority to deal with land-use issues. That's a local decision."

Several weeks after Cox expressed his fears, state and local officials gave owners approval to rebuild. They did so even though the state's construction control line, beyond which no development is allowed, was now more than 100 feet offshore.

Eighteen months later, many of the 41 owners have rebuilt or are in the process of rebuilding. Some, such as Gail Leacy of Mobile, Ala., relied on flood insurance. Leacy collected about $60,000 to make repairs after an ocean-front house that had been ripped from its pilings slammed into her bayside vacation home.

"It was a combination of homeowners' and flood, mostly flood," she said.

Georges was the third hurricane to damage Leacy's house. Hurricane Elena struck in 1985 while the house was being built. Opal tore a hole in her roof in 1995.

"You get pretty discouraged after a while," Leacy said. "But then you get it all fixed up and go down there, and it's absolutely beautiful."

In all, FEMA approved 278 claims of Dauphin Island property owners worth nearly $4 million after Georges — an average of $14,352 per claim.

Since 1978, owners have filed more than 2,300 claims, totaling $16.9 million, or $7,335 per claim. About 70 percent of the 1,500 island properties are second homes or rentals. The average yearly flood premium is $482.

Even some Dauphin Island officials question whether federally backed flood insurance ought to be available for vacation homes.

"I really don't think the [program] was set up to insure rental property or someone's second income," said Alma Wagner, a council member.

Hawking flood insurance

Though it may seem odd for the federal government to hawk insurance for vacation properties, FEMA is not shy about its marketing efforts. It encourages agents to sell policies to property owners who live outside flood-prone areas.

"Think you'll never be flooded because you don't live near water or live high on a hill? Just listen to the news. Experts report that weather patterns are changing fast, and so are your chances of being flooded," a FEMA advertisement states.

Since 1995, FEMA has targeted millions of Americans with television, radio, and

Hurricanes Dominate Insurance Losses

Among private insurers, hurricanes accounted for $3 of every $4 spent on natural disasters from 1950 to 1992. In total, insurers spent $42.5 billion during this time.

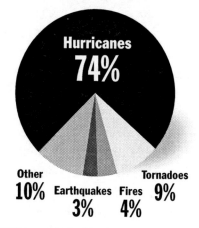

Hurricanes
74%

Other
10% **Earthquakes** **Fires** **Tornadoes**
3% **4%** **9%**

SOURCE: Insurance Services Offices Inc.

direct-mail advertising, at a cost of $55 million from policy fees.

Tens of thousands of new policies have been sold,

pushing the number of Americans with flood insurance to more than 4.1 million.

By selling more flood insurance, especially to less-risky properties, FEMA is better able to cover its losses. The agency says it makes money on all but its subsidized policies. It also stresses that only one of every four houses in floodplains is insured.

The agency has prepared ad slicks and counter cards and established an insurance leads program so that 26,000 private agents can get sales leads by fax or phone. Under its co-op advertising program, companies can save up to 50 percent on costs — but only 25 percent if they include information about private insurance they sell. The flood program even has an award — the Administrator's Cup, which goes annually to the company posting the biggest sales gain.

When Congress passed the flood insurance act, it faced a quandary. In order to sign up older houses most likely to be flooded, it had to offer attractive rates. But if it based those rates on standard insurance principles, charging enough to cover losses and build a reserve for catastrophes, premiums would be so high that no one would buy coverage.

Congress solved this dilemma by subsidizing the most vulnerable properties. Their owners would get steep discounts, paying about one-third of their actual risks, while owners of new houses paid full rates. Over time, the riskier properties would be replaced by newer houses, and the program would achieve financial stability. At least that was the idea.

Thirty years later, nearly one-third of all properties are still subsidized. And a 1998 FEMA study estimated that those buildings might not be weeded out of the program until 2050.

"When you've got 30 percent of your properties paying only 38 percent of their full risk, there isn't a lot of room to adjust," FEMA's Pasterick said.

He said the flood program had suffered an average annual shortfall of $450 million by failing to charge subsidized properties rates based on their actual risks. That's $2.25 billion in the last five years that could have gone to build reserves.

"It's the subsidies that are killing the program," said H. Joseph Coughlin, flood program specialist.

Since 1995, the flood program has had to borrow $1 billion from the Treasury to pay bills associated with hurricanes and Midwest floods.

From time to time, FEMA has proposed adding surcharges and placing restrictions on subsidized properties. Each time, Congress refused, contending it was "inconsistent" with the program's intent.

In 1994, a congressional panel asked FEMA to study the effect of raising rates for subsidized properties. The agency hired an accounting firm, which delivered a report in early 1999. A year later, the report is still being studied. FEMA declined to make the report available.

One fear is that charging actuarial rates would drive high-risk properties from the flood program. Some of those properties' owners would then turn to FEMA for disaster aid after storms. And that would push disaster costs even higher as FEMA faces pressures to cut spending.

Properties that benefit from subsidized rates account for a disproportionate share of houses damaged time and again.

FEMA calls these "repetitive-loss properties." They are buildings with at least two claims exceeding $1,000 in a 10-

year period. Since 1978, owners of more than 75,000 such properties have filed $2.8 billion in claims.

That means just 2 percent of National Flood Insurance Program properties nationwide account for nearly one-third of the program's $8.6 billion in claims. About 96 percent of the 35,000 repetitive-loss properties still in the program enjoy subsidized rates.

Historically, those properties tended to be located along rivers and levees. That trend began to shift in the 1990s, as hurricanes and coastal storms took their toll on states that had undergone unprecedented development. Florida, New Jersey and North Carolina now rank among the top losers.

Vulnerable Jersey Shore

The problem is particularly acute along the Jersey Shore.

Half of all flood claims in the state's four coastal counties, totaling $131 million, involve buildings with two or more losses. Those 3,887 properties account for nearly one-third of the $403 million in flood claims statewide.

Sixteen beach towns in New Jersey rank among the top 200 communities nationwide with multiple losses. Homeowners in those towns have made 7,831 claims, totaling $88.2 million since 1978, an average claim of $11,262.

Ocean City accounts for $11.2 million of those losses, ranking 18th nationally.

"It's all part of living on an island where the elevation doesn't exceed 11 feet anywhere," said Kit Wright, Ocean City environmental officer. "If we get a storm with a full moon, we're in trouble."

The city is taking steps to lessen flood damage, elevating a dozen buildings, paid for with federal tax dollars. But even as some buildings are removed, others are added. Wright recently got an updated list of repetitive-loss properties from FEMA. "There must be 100 new sheets in there," she said with a sigh.

FEMA is spending millions to raise private properties. Some of the resorts that benefit are among the richest beach towns in America, including Malibu, Calif., and Westport, Conn.

Since 1994, Westport has received $776,000 to elevate 19 flood-prone houses along Long Island Sound. Recently, FEMA awarded it $500,000 to waterproof private homes, study ways to reduce downtown flooding, and raffle off a Hurricane Home Makeover to a lucky resident.

The town of expansive Cape Cods and sprawling mansions has one of the highest median household incomes in America — $90,518 in 1996, or three times the national average. Houses sell for an average $660,000. In all, the town's property is worth $6.6 billion.

Westport's tax rate — 1 percent of the value of a home — is among the lowest in the nation. So why did it need federal help?

"Citizens in the U.S., irrespective of their ability to pay, have the right to relief," said Diane Goss Farrell, Westport's top elected official. "The fact that Westport is a wealthy community is less important than the fact it is a coastal community."

State officials, not FEMA, decide which houses are elevated.

"It's pure fantasy to think that these towns are going to raise their own taxes to pay when federal money is available," said Douglas Glowacki, a Connecticut planning official.

Now, Congress and FEMA want to up the ante. Last summer, lawmakers proposed spending $200 million more to elevate flood-prone buildings. Owners who agree to elevate would have 75 percent of the cost paid by taxpayers. Those who refuse would be charged actuarial rates.

Federal officials say elevating the houses would cut flood losses. "It makes good sense to do this," FEMA's Witt said.

But owners of many coastal properties have already elevated on their own, and flood losses keep rising, doubling in the 1990s to more than $5 billion.

Nor is elevation a sure way to prevent damage. As coastlines erode and sea levels rise, homes that appear safe today will become vulnerable in a generation or two, coastal experts say.

"We're already finding that some of the building setbacks we established in North Carolina were not nearly enough," said Courtney Hackney, member of a state board overseeing coastal development. "Elevating isn't going to save you if the ocean is at your doorstep."

Federal effort let homeowners seize on an unintended opportunity

In 1988, Congress passed the Upton-Jones Act, offering taxpayer help to move flood-prone properties out of harm's way. The rationale was that it would be cheaper to move or demolish houses than continue paying disaster aid and flood claims.

But at a nearly $28 million, the program cost taxpayers far more than claims would have, federal investigators said. And some owners with large enough lots used the program to demolish older, less valuable houses and replace them with larger beach homes.

Congress agreed to pay owners to demolish their houses under the assumption that most of the lots would be left empty.

Some owners who received the demolition fees did not tear down their beach houses. Instead they sold them to enterprising middlemen, who purchased salvage rights and carted them off whole.

Thus, the Federal Emergency Management Agency paid demolition fees for houses that were actually moved. And it was all perfectly legal.

"I wouldn't gamble 25 cents on a slot machine. But on a piece of land, I'll take a chance," said Malcolm Fearing, a developer and insurance broker in Manteo, N.C., who said he bought salvage rights for 12 to 15 houses.

"I'd bid low. Maybe $2,000 to $4,000. Of course, I had to pay to move the house. That could be substantial."

Fearing moved two houses down the beach. He carted the others to Manteo, where he now rents them. "Upton-Jones was a good program," he said. "Theoretically, it was a good program."

A 1993 audit by FEMA's inspector general found that most of the demolition claims were for houses that had not been seriously damaged. In one sample, 18 of 24 owners chose to demolish their houses and receive payment, even though their lots were deep enough to move the houses back. The owners then built larger houses, "substantially increasing their investment and rental income," the report said.

A bigger problem: Very few owners of endangered properties participated. They considered their oceanfront properties too valuable.

Not a single property owner along New Jersey's 109-

mile developed shoreline took a buyout or moved back, out of harm's way, records show.

By comparison, 20 houses were demolished or moved in Pennsylvania, most atop the bluffs of Lake Erie.

In 1994, Congress killed the program. Since then, FEMA has acquired thousands of flood-prone properties using other funds — but nearly all of them have been inland. It has been unable to buy many coastal properties for a simple reason: They cost too much.

A taste of the beach

By the reckoning of the federal flood insurance program, the house that Michael Schuldt bought last year in Center City is in the middle of a floodplain.

So to get a federally backed mortgage, Schuldt had to buy federal flood insurance — at the same base rate as many homeowners in Ocean City, N.J.

Never mind that Schuldt's property, on 26th Street between Pine and Lombard Streets near the Schuylkill, is a long way from the ocean. Government flood maps say it has a one-in-four chance of flooding every 25 years.

"It's not like we're right on the river's edge," Schuldt said. "And it's not like there's been a flood around here recently."

Center City has not had a serious flood since Hurricane Diane in 1955. And despite record rain dumped by Hurricane Floyd in September, there was no major damage downtown.

"It was a really good test. We didn't get one drop," Schuldt said.

But according to the Federal Emergency Management Agency, Schuldt's risk of flooding is no less than that of many property owners right on the beach.

Schuldt said he paid $680 a year for his flood coverage. "It was actually close to what we were paying for home-owners' insurance. It was a nice little shock."

His insurance rate is as high as in some beach towns because FEMA groups properties by flood zones, based on their overall risk. Whether that zone is on the beach or in an inland city does not matter.

Schuldt suspects that he is helping to subsidize lower premiums for some beachfront properties. His premium is higher than the average in all but six beach resorts on the Jersey Shore, records show.

But when it comes to filing flood claims, Ocean City has a lot more action than Center City.

Since 1978, Philadelphians have filed 371 claims under the national flood program. Property owners in Ocean City have submitted nearly 10 times that number — 3,580.

In outdated maps, a poor primer on risk

DESTIN, Fla. — After Hurricane Opal engulfed the Florida Panhandle in October 1995, causing nearly $400 million in flood losses, engineers from the Federal Emergency Management Agency took a hard look at how accurately their maps captured the flood risk in this boom-ing resort.

What they found was disturbing. The maps bore little resemblance to the actual risk. In some areas, the storm surge was five feet higher than what the agency had expected in a hurricane the size of Opal.

"Opal was a wake-up call," said Darryl Hatheway, an engineer who worked with FEMA on the map evaluations.

"High water from Opal ranged from 8 to 20 feet. The flood maps were showing elevations from 5 to 12."

FEMA's maps are often outdated or wrong, interviews and documents show. Nearly half of the agency's 100,000 drawings are at least a decade old — a lifetime for volatile, flood-prone shorelines. Many are based on estimates, not detailed engineering studies. And some do not include recent building along the coast.

As a result, local officials who rely on the maps to regulate development are approving projects without knowing the real risks, placing property in harm's way and increasing the likelihood of costly flood losses.

"In the coastal setting, there's more of a need for constant updating," said Michael K. Buckley, who oversees FEMA's. maps. "It's very dynamic."

State and local officials use the maps to plan for hurricanes and storms, including identifying evacuation routes. The maps also play a key role in determining flood insurance rates. If they understate the flood risk, owners pay less — in effect, a hidden subsidy.

But even when FEMA knows the real risks, its policies perpetuate subsidies.

Say the agency's maps show an oceanfront home with a low risk of flooding. Then a hurricane swamps the home, causing thousands of dollars in damages. FEMA redraws its maps to reflect the increased risk. But instead of having to pay more, the owner gets to keep the cheaper insurance rate.

An agency document explains: "If you have insurance before the new maps take effect, the basis for rating that policy remains unchanged."

Under this grandfather clause, owners are entitled to the rates in place when their houses were built. A homeowner can maintain that rate and save a lot of money, said Bob Durrin, an agency flood specialist.

Now, suppose a property owner's risk of flooding decreases after FEMA revises its maps. His rate is not grandfathered. Under the agency's rules, he gets to apply for a lower rate.

After FEMA revised its maps in Destin and other gulf resorts, local officials and homeowners complained that the new, more accurate drawings would depress property values.

"There was some fear ... mostly for homes built before Opal that now were shown in areas that flooded," said Robert P. Francke, Destin's development director. "My main concern is that I have maps that don't reflect what's out there."

FEMA two years ago asked Congress for $900 million to update its flood maps — the world's second-largest collection after the military's — and shift from paper to digital maps available over the Internet. But Congress rejected a proposal to levy a $15 charge on all new U.S. mortgages. Now the agency proposes charging fees to commercial users of the maps to generate $100 million a year.

The changes can't come too soon for some.

In Ocean Shores, Wash., clerks in the building department found the flood map so hard to read that they stuck it in a drawer. When a reporter asked what they used, a clerk showed him another map tacked to a wall in the rear office. It was 20 years old.

"But at least we can read it," the clerk said.

Part 5

In defense of
Jersey's shores

For Army engineers, the Atlantic is an indomitable enemy

LONG BRANCH, N.J. — In its campaign for a piece of the nation's $40 billion business-conference market, the renovated Ocean Place Conference Resort has added an impressive arsenal of amenities.

The hotel has 254 guest rooms, all with water-view balconies. It boasts a million-dollar office center, heated pools, and a spa featuring full-body seaweed and mud masks.

And it offers something that was not part of the hotel's recent $10 million renovation plan — a brand-new, manicured beach to defend its investment from coastal storms and hurricanes.

That came courtesy of taxpayers.

It was the product of the U.S. Army Corps of Engineers, the same Corps that built Fort McHenry on Baltimore Harbor and swept the minefields of Normandy Beach on D-Day.

Over the last 220 years, the Corps has helped defend America's shores from foreign invaders. Today, it is pumping sand to defend hotels, vacation homes, amusement piers and fudge shops from the surging ocean.

In that role it finds itself in the heat of another battle.

Taxpayer-funded beachfill has become a symbol in the debate over coastal development, even though it is only one in a matrix of federal subsidies that benefit beach towns and property owners.

Most beachfills are "pork barrel" projects, says Lim

Vallianos, a 30-year veteran of the Corps who is now an engineering consultant. Politicians — not engineers or geologists — decide which beaches to fill, and for the most part the projects protect investment properties.

"John Q. Public pays for the protection of commercial enterprises," Vallianos said.

Where beachfill is available, states and towns have less incentive to force builders to keep away from the fragile shoreline. And with so much investment at stake, coastal experts agree that beach towns will have to keep replenishing their beaches.

But with sea levels rising, it will take more and more sand — and billions more dollars — to hold the line in front of the developed shoreline for decades to come. And costs will increase as offshore sand supplies dwindle.

The debate centers on who should pay and, more fundamentally, whether it is worth the expense.

At its core is the tension between engineers, who view nature as a problem to be solved, and geologists, who hold that engineers cannot see beyond the life span of a mortgage.

The engineers, with the support of developers and local officials, hold that with so much valuable property on the coasts, the nation has no choice but to save the beaches.

"Retreat from the Shore is the most nonsensical discussion I ever heard," asserts James Mancini, longtime mayor of Long Beach Township. "Let's say the Shore is the boundary of the United States of America, the greatest country in the world. We have to protect it, and anybody with any brains agrees with that."

"Are you just going to walk away from the Eastern Seaboard of the United States and say it doesn't exist?"

ELIZABETH V. ROBERTSON / Inquirer Suburban Staff
A photo held by Lou Davis of Simpson Avenue in Ocean City, N.J.,
shows flooding along his street in 1992.

asks Hank Glazier, the head of the Ocean City Boardwalk
Merchants Association.

The geologists, backed by environmentalists, counter
that beaches are never endangered — only beachfront
properties. Erosion is erratic and unpredictable, and they
say it is only a matter of time before rising tides turn
today's beaches into tomorrow's sea bottoms. Thus, beachfill is a permanent and costly commitment.

"Engineering just never stops," said Orrin H. Pilkey, a
Duke University geologist who is viewed as the antichrist
by the engineering community.

The initial pumping operation is only the beginning.

The offshore dredge that pumps the sand has to return to refill the beach every three to six years. Projects require a 50-year commitment of sand, and no one knows what will happen at the end of that time.

"Beachfill isn't like building a bridge," said Jeff Gebert of the Corps' Philadelphia district. "You don't build it and walk away expecting that there isn't anything you have to do for the next 10 years or 20 years."

Corps records are incomplete, but a review of annual reports and other documents dating to 1956 shows that the agency has spent at least $1.4 billion on shore-protection projects, in today's dollars. Adding state and local shares, the figure grows to more than $2.2 billion.

The ongoing fill project in North Jersey represents an escalation in the Corps' battle with nature. At 21 miles, from Sea Bright to Manasquan, it is the largest beachfill project in the nation's history.

If fully funded over 50 years, the $1 billion federal share of the costs would rival the total spent in the history of the program to date. About $5 billion would be required to defend the entire developed Jersey shoreline in the next 50 years; and tens of billions more to hold sandy beaches in front of developed areas nationwide.

Who foots the bill?

The Clinton administration has stated that it wants the federal government to get out of the beachfill business.

But as development has increased, so has the demand for beachfill — and pressure from lobbyists. In the last five years, Congress has appropriated $461 million for shore protection. That is well more than a third of the federal money spent in the 43-year lifetime of the program.

One reason the sand has kept flowing is Howard Marlowe. Working out of a Washington office, the former

Senate staffer has become the nation's premier coastal lobbyist. When Marlowe's newly formed American Coastal Coalition convened a conference in 1998, it drew the U.S. Army Corps of Engineers' top-ranking civilian; five U.S. senators; a long list of state and municipal officials; and two White House staffers.

Lobbyists such as Marlowe and New Jersey's Kenneth Smith hold that the nation's eroding beaches are "infrastructure" that should be maintained like man-made highways. It is a popular defense of beachfill, along with the argument that the U.S. government should be as generous to resort towns as it is to flood-prone river towns, where people live and work year-round.

That's an argument questioned even by some Corps officials, who believe resort towns should pay more.

In a typical project, the federal government picks up 65 percent of the total; the states, 25 percent; and municipalities 10 percent or less. The biggest beneficiaries — beachfront property owners — contribute indirectly through property taxes and a portion of the same taxes paid by all Americans.

"If you're the homeowner on the beach, it's a great deal," said Courtney Hackney, a coastal regulator in North Carolina, "because you pay very little for it. If you're a citizen living in Ohio, it's probably not a good deal at all."

James R. Houston, the Corps' chief engineer and one of the nation's leading proponents of beach nourishment, said that questions over who should pay are legitimate.

"The person who lives right on the coast, it seems like maybe they ought to pay more than somebody that lives inland or lives in the middle of the state," he said at a 1998 forum in Texas.

Fuller Brush men

Officially, the Corps has declared neutrality in the debate over beachfill appropriations. However, Corps officials, such as Houston, have appeared at coastal-development conferences and have openly encouraged local and state politicians and developers to lobby for projects.

The Corps does not undertake cost and feasibility studies until local governments apply for projects; thus, in effect, towns and counties have to make the first move.

Dery Bennett, president of the American Littoral Society, an environmental group, said Corps representatives have tried to sell New Jersey towns on beachfill like so many "Fuller Brush men. It's common knowledge that they're proactive in selling their wares," he said.

That is something of a reversal. In the early days, Corps officials wanted no part of shore protection and became involved only at the behest of Congress. "Not a damn one of these guys thought the federal government should be involved in it," Vallianos said.

The Corps' first foray into shore protection occurred more than 200 years ago, and it had nothing to do with pumping sand.

After it was created by Congress on March 11, 1779, the Corps went to work fortifying the shores of the new nation. It built Fort McHenry, where Francis Scott Key wrote "The Star Spangled Banner." Corps members were in every major war, and were part of the D-Day invasion on June 6, 1944.

But by then, the Corps had been drafted into a very different mission on the domestic front: defending America's beaches from nature.

In the 1920s, the Corps viewed beaches as a problem

for the states, and the protection of waterfront property as no business of the United States, said Albert E. Cowdrey, a Corps historian.

But beach-erosion studies by engineers in New Jersey in 1922 and 1924 spawned the American Shore and Beach Preservation Association, the nation's first beach-lobbying group. It pressured Congress to deploy the Corps, arguing that beaches were a national concern because Shore visitors came from many states.

The lobbyists prevailed. In the 1930s, Congress passed the Rivers and Harbors Act, commissioning the Corps to fight erosion. Thus an arm of the Defense Department was officially enlisted in the battle of the beaches.

The nation's first sand-pumping project began on Coney Island in 1922, but the Corps did not undertake its first project until the 1950s, and did not become heavily involved in beachfill until after the Ash Wednesday Storm of 1962 that pummeled the Mid-Atlantic.

Over the next 37 years, it would leave an extraordinary mark on America's beaches.

The data game

No one is certain how much sand Corps contractors have pumped onto the nation's beaches — not even the Corps.

"There is no funding mechanism to maintain a national database," a 1993 Corps report stated.

Pilkey, the Duke University geologist, contends that the Corps has used the data gaps to its advantage, making exaggerated claims about the durability of pumped sand and the accuracy of the computer models that tell it how much sand to pump. He said the Corps has placed too much faith in models that might work out fine in wave tanks but do not hold up in the violent and chaotic real world of the oceans.

While the Corps contends that its projects have performed as predicted, in the 1993 paper it acknowledged that the lack of data makes it difficult to assess.

"This lack-of-records excuse just blows my mind," Pilkey said.

By its own admission, the Corps has made costly mistakes, and as a result, taxpayers have spent millions to repair beaches, jetties and groins — and now stand to spend millions more.

A bungled Corps project led to a breach that swallowed more than 200 houses on Long Island in the winter of 1992-93. On Assateague Island, across from Ocean City, Md., Corps jetties completed in 1934 have accelerated erosion that is ripping apart the north end of the national seashore.

Still, even Pilkey acknowledges that Corps projects have prevented property damage, and that beachfill is a far more benign strategy than hardened seawalls. Without beachfill, "Wrightsville Beach [N.C.] would have disappeared over the horizon a long time ago," Pilkey said.

Like almost all of the Corps' major projects, the Wrightsville beachfill is defending private property. The Corps disputes claims that its projects encourage development, but it does not dispute that its primary mission is to guard real estate and the infrastructure that supports it.

To qualify for funding, projects have to be justified on the basis of preventing flood damage to private and public property. Thus, federal policies "virtually limit shore-protection projects to densely developed areas with high economic value," the Corps said in a 1995 report.

For example, the Corps has pumped more than $42 million worth of sand on built-out Ocean City, Md. Yet it has been unable to secure funding for a major fill project on undeveloped Assateague, across the channel.

Undeveloped Island Beach State Park is the only portion of the Jersey Shore that is not under consideration for federal beachfill money.

In its project planning, the Corps does not take into account the most catastrophic storms — a fact that could prove expensive.

"This project is not designed for a '62 storm," said Anthony Ciorra, the project manager for the North Jersey beachfill. Such a storm could erase mass quantities of sand and cause serious flood damage.

"One storm, not terribly unusual, could wipe out our investment here virtually overnight," Vallianos said. He added that a major failure on such a visible and expensive project might drive the Corps out of the beachfill business.

"If an Ash Wednesday Storm came along, to me it might spell doom for that program," he said.

Ultimately, the erosion problem transcends engineering, said Gary Griggs, director of the University of California's marine-science institute in Santa Cruz. The oceans, he points out, are thousands of miles wide.

"Here we are protecting inches," he said. "We can't protect ourselves from every natural disaster."

"Erecting a building on a beach is like building on an active volcano," Vallianos said. "You take your chances, and, sooner or later, you lose."

When beach projects cause damage

The Army Corps of Engineers expects to spend hundreds of millions in taxpayer dollars to fix environmental damage that the Corps concedes was caused by some of its own projects.

"The Corps has caused so much damage in so many places," said Orrin H. Pilkey, a Duke University geologist. "Geologists are surprised more people haven't picked up on this."

Ironically, engineering mistakes might keep the Corps — and U.S. taxpayers — in the sand-pumping business. Jetties have caused erosion all over the country, and lob-

Washaway Beaches

■ **Cape Cod, Mass.** Wellfleet, Eastham and Orleans have lost up to 2 percent of their lands in the last century; Marion, on Buzzards Bay, 3 percent. Geologists cite rising sea levels and sinking land.

■ **Sandbridge, Va.** Seawalls and $8 million worth of pumped sand have failed to stop erosion, which has continued at a rate of up to 10 feet a year.

■ **Fort Lauderdale, Fla.** In a popular recreation area, the city is losing 5 feet of beach a year. The state says that jetties built to stabilize Port Everglades are interrupting sand flow. Inlets cause 85 percent of erosion in Florida.

■ **Grand Isle, La.** The 200 miles of barrier islands, which protect the mainland from storms and saltwater intrusion, are vanishing at a rate of 35 feet a year. The Chandeleur Islands alone lost 145 feet to Hurricane Georges.

■ **San Diego** Beaches and bluffs in San Diego County are disappearing at a rate of up to 8 feet a year. Rivers are no longer delivering sediment to the beaches.

■ **Washaway Beach, Wash.** Appropriately named, the sparsely populated area is literally washing away. At 100 feet a year, it is believed to have the highest erosion rate in America.

byists are pushing Congress for millions in beach repairs that the Corps, always looking for work, is ready to make.

A few examples of engineering gone awry:

Long Island. After the Ash Wednesday Storm of 1962 ripped apart Long Island, the Corps planned to build 21 sand-trapping groins in the hard-hit Westhampton Dunes area. Against its better judgment, it bowed to pressure from local property owners and politicians and altered the project, completing only 15. In the next two decades, erosion accelerated, culminating in a mile-wide breach that swallowed 200 houses in the stormy winter of 1992-93. The property owners sued the U.S. government and won. The Corps then stitched together the breach with an 1,800-foot steel wall buried under 8 feet of pumped sand. It will cost taxpayers $100 million to keep the beach filled for the next 30 years.

Cape May. From 1908 to 1911, the U.S. government spent $15 million to build mile-long stone jetties to stabilize the inlet between the Wildwoods and Cape May. Once finished, the beaches in the Wildwoods began expanding, while Cape May's virtually disappeared. Today, Cape May has a beach, but only because of the largesse of U.S. taxpayers. Because the erosion was caused by a Corps project, the taxpayers are picking up 90 percent of the cost of a $150 million, 50-year fill.

Barnegat Inlet. In 1940, the Corps built two mile-long jetties at the northern end of Long Beach Island to stabilize the channel that connects the Atlantic Ocean with Barnegat Bay. Together, they formed an arrowhead. But the currents threw the jetties a curve, and sand began clogging the channel. The Army determined that the angled south jetty had to be straightened. That project was completed in 1992 — at a cost of at least $40 million. The channel requires constant dredging, and the new alignment has been blamed for accelerating erosion at the bay side of Island Beach State Park.

Assateague. A 1933 hurricane ripped a channel between Ocean City, Md., and Assateague, which had shared the same sandy spit. The Corps installed stone jetties to stabilize the new inlet. But the rock walls interrupted the currents of sand that supplied Assateague's beaches, and the new island started narrowing and moving west. Today, Assateague is set off from the old spit like a badly broken bone. The Atlantic shoreline of the island is about 2,000 feet west of Ocean City's shoreline. The north end of the island is losing about 30 feet of beach a year. The Corps has agreed to pump sand on the island, but has been unable to secure congressional funding.

On the Jersey Shore, a perpetual battle with erosion

More than any state in the nation, New Jersey has taken a stand against the invading tides. It has the most engineered beach in the country, its coastline bearing more scar tissue than any other shoreline.

It has one of the nation's highest annual shore-protection budgets, $25 million, administered by the state's land-use agency, the Department of Environmental Protection.

The state is so committed to shoring up its beaches that the department's commissioner, Robert Shinn has lobbied in Trenton and Washington for beachfill money.

Today, buffering shore towns from the endless assault of the Atlantic Ocean are 483 sand-trapping groins, 23 miles of seawalls and bulkheads, and an assortment of wave-breakers, sandbags, Geotubes, Beachsaver Reefs

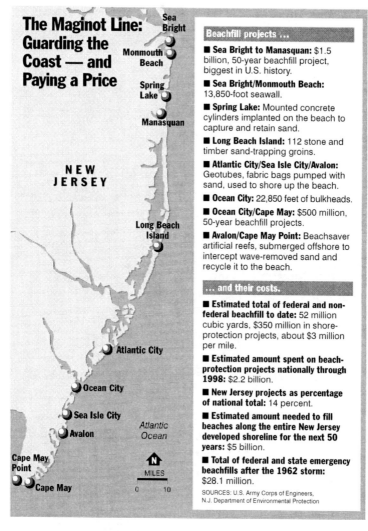

The Maginot Line: Guarding the Coast — and Paying a Price

Sea Bright
Monmouth Beach
Spring Lake
Manasquan

NEW JERSEY

Long Beach Island

Atlantic City

Ocean City

Sea Isle City

Avalon

Cape May Point

Cape May

Atlantic Ocean

MILES
0   10

Beachfill projects ...

■ **Sea Bright to Manasquan:** $1.5 billion, 50-year beachfill project, biggest in U.S. history.

■ **Sea Bright/Monmouth Beach:** 13,850-foot seawall.

■ **Spring Lake:** Mounted concrete cylinders implanted on the beach to capture and retain sand.

■ **Long Beach Island:** 112 stone and timber sand-trapping groins.

■ **Atlantic City/Sea Isle City/Avalon:** Geotubes, fabric bags pumped with sand, used to shore up the beach.

■ **Ocean City:** 22,850 feet of bulkheads.

■ **Ocean City/Cape May:** $500 million, 50-year beachfill projects.

■ **Avalon/Cape May Point:** Beachsaver artificial reefs, submerged offshore to intercept wave-removed sand and recycle it to the beach.

... and their costs.

■ **Estimated total of federal and non-federal beachfill to date:** 52 million cubic yards, $350 million in shore-protection projects, about $3 million per mile.

■ **Estimated amount spent on beach-protection projects nationally through 1998:** $2.2 billion.

■ **New Jersey projects as percentage of national total:** 14 percent.

■ **Estimated amount needed to fill beaches along the entire New Jersey developed shoreline for the next 50 years:** $5 billion.

■ **Total of federal and state emergency beachfills after the 1962 storm:** $28.1 million.

SOURCES: U.S. Army Corps of Engineers, N.J. Department of Environmental Protection

and other devices.

From the great stone wall of Sea Bright to the reefs off Cape May Point — dedicated by Gov. Whitman herself five years ago — an Inquirer analysis shows that in the last 50 years, federal and state taxpayers have spent at least $600 million to protect coastal real estate. Most of that is investment property.

"Our obligation should be toward protecting the people," said Norbert P. Psuty, a Rutgers University geologist, "but should we be protecting their investments?"

It won't get any cheaper. The state has turned to beach-fill as its prime weapon against erosion. But erosion is an endless process compounded by frequent storms, rising sea level, and dwindling supplies of sand — not to mention other engineering projects.

Taxpayers have committed $2 billion to pump sand on New Jersey beaches for the next 50 years. That cost could rise to $5 billion if other proposed beachfill projects come to fruition.

In Ocean City, which might be the coastal engineering capital of the United States, the state and federal governments plan to spend $350 million over the next 50 years.

For better or for worse, New Jersey is the prototype for coastal engineering nationwide.

For thousands of years, shorelines have ebbed and flowed, and barrier islands have moved, re-formed and disappeared.

Only in the last 150 years has this become a problem.

Until the late 17th century, the Jersey Shore was mostly deserted. In the 1850s, the railroads forever changed the Shore, bringing visitors and investors. Sea Isle City, uninhabited in 1850, had 300 cottages and 30 hotels by 1900.

Erosion was now a threat.

"Beach erosion as a problem exists only where development has taken place," noted the New Jersey Shore Protection Master Plan of 1981, the last one published by the state. It chided developers for exacerbating that problem by leveling dunes to clear land and provide oceanfront views.

Where the ocean meets the mainland, rising seas and

sinking lands work in tandem to erode beaches. But barrier islands, such as those along the fragile chain from Long Beach Island to Cape May Point, are not eroding so much as re-forming.

As they are inundated by rising seas and storm waves, they literally move back from the encroaching ocean, toward the land. That's how they stay above water.

New Jersey's beaches are frequently pocked with peat, the remnants of old marshes that once were on the bay side of the islands. Periodically, storm waves peel away layers of sand to reveal tree stumps.

During storms, waves smash the beach and drag sand out to sea. As the waves advance landward over the flattened beachfront, they join forces with strong onshore winds to drive some of the sand westward, toward the mainland. In this way, the island rebuilds itself.

Under ordinary circumstances, as sea level rises, Seven Mile Island might migrate ever so slowly toward the mainland.

However, Avalon and Stone Harbor, located on the island, are not going anywhere soon. They have been anchored in place by $3 billion worth of real estate, and both towns are waiting for a 50-year federal beachfill project such as the one in Ocean City.

For Ocean City, it is just the latest in a long history of fills.

According to records of the state and the Army Corps of Engineers, more than 15 million cubic yards of sand have been dumped or pumped on the city's five miles of beaches since the 1950s. That represents close to one-third of all the sand ever placed on the state's beaches. Virtually every block of beach fronts a bulkhead, and 50 groins — giant sand clamps of stone and timber — stripe the beach, one every few blocks.

"They're at war with the sea," Psuty said.

Until 1982, the city had its own dredge and was drawing sand from the bay. It undertook 12 major projects between 1970 and 1982. In the 1990s, the Army came to the rescue.

With the intervention of an influential congressman, William Hughes, who happened to live in Ocean City, the town secured a 50-year federal project covering virtually the entire beach.

Ocean City's future has not been secured, however. Like all Corps projects, Ocean City's will last 50 years only if funding is available, and those decisions are made year to year. The same is true in North Jersey. Even if fully funded, the projects might be little more than very costly Band-Aids.

The wild and chaotic episodes that characterize erosion are embedded in a larger and incontrovertible trend: The oceans are slowly drowning the shorelines.

The oceans worldwide have been swelling since the end of the most recent ice age, about 12,000 years ago, the result of melting glaciers, sinking land masses, and shifts in the Earth's crust.

In the last 100 years, sea level has risen 16 inches, according to measurements at the Atlantic City tidal gauge.

Controversy continues over whether the rate will accelerate because of human-enhanced global warming. But even at current rates, a little more than an inch every seven years, the rising waters are an ever-growing threat to coastal property.

The waters along the Jersey coast are seven inches higher than they were when the Shore was ravaged by a

JOHN COSTELLO / Inquirer Staff Photographer

Crews worked to fortify the shore in Strathmere, N.J., in early 1998.

1944 hurricane.

At today's levels, the five high tides during the devastating 1962 Ash Wednesday Storm each would have been five inches higher, resulting in more flooding and more wave power. Wave force increases with height in such a way that a four-foot wave is about twice as powerful as a three-foot wave.

In short, Psuty said, a 100-year storm is not what it used to be.

It's a 30-year storm.

"We're tripling the recurrence intervals," he said.

Even Shinn acknowledges that someday the state may have to be less ambitious in its shore-protection program. "You can't do this forever," he said. "But in the reasonable future our plan is a realistic one."

Part 6

===

In New Jersey and elsewhere, back bays under seige

Vacation homes as far as the eye can see

STAFFORD TOWNSHIP, N.J. — The houses looming above Barnegat Bay on Mill Creek Road form a wall of development that would rival any suburban boomtown. As far as the eye can see, expensive vacation homes and year-round residences tuck shoulder to shoulder on what was once a pristine salt marsh.

The marsh was dredged and filled decades ago. Developers carved lagoons and built modestly priced vacation cottages. Over time, the houses got bigger and more expensive as development pushed closer to the water. The coves and tidal channels that had been home to a rich assortment of waterfowl, fish and crabs took on a new look.

Sprawl had arrived at the back bay.

These days, it is hard to catch a glimpse of Barnegat Bay while driving along Mill Creek Road and dozens of other streets like it up and down the coast. The shimmering water is out there, all right. But increasingly it is being eclipsed as building pressures shift from the barrier islands to the back bays.

"The irony is that the very thing that probably attracted people in the first place is being lost," says William deCamp Jr., president of Save Barnegat Bay, a nonprofit group. "The sense of place and heritage and the wonderful views, all of the things that make this area so special, are being sold off to the highest bidder."

Stafford Township is one of the towns at the center of this new coastal battleground. Once a backwater on the way to the beach, it is now struggling to accommodate a rapid influx of newcomers and developers, while preserving the area's unique identity and fragile resources.

"It's happening so fast, it's scary," says John Spodofora, a councilman and longtime resident, touring the Mill Creek area.

All along America's coasts, wherever fresh water mixes with the ocean to form biologically rich bays and sounds, unprecedented development pressures are threatening to overwhelm the back bays.

In Maryland, environmental groups are bracing for a new development boom in the watershed bordering Chesapeake Bay. The area is expected to add three million people in the next 15 years. "We've barely been able to hold our own up until now," said Michael Shultz, spokesman for the Chesapeake Bay Foundation.

In North Carolina, more than 20,000 acres of prime shellfish beds have been closed due to pollution in the Albemarle-Pamlico Sounds. Unsafe levels of mercury and dioxin have been found in fish, PCBs and heavy metals in sediments. Recently, developers took advantage of a regulatory loophole, building on approximately 15,000 acres of wetlands in New Hanover County.

Environmentalists fear that the floodwaters of Hurricane Floyd in September delivered a toxic brew of agricultural fertilizers and animal wastes to the sounds and bays dotting the Carolina coast, draining oxygen, giving rise to algal blooms, and killing off fish and shellfish.

In California, building has claimed most of the tidal marshes surrounding the San Francisco Bay. In Texas, only 15 percent of Galveston Bay's sea grass meadows remain.

From Buzzards Bay in Massachusetts to Tampa Bay in Florida, runoff from coastal sprawl, inadequate sewage

JOHN COSTELLO / Inquirer Staff Photographer
Homes are squeezed along the waterfront in Stafford Township, N.J.

Development, Back Bays and Water Quality

Across America, state officials and environmental groups are struggling to deal with the effects of increased development along the back bays. Here are some examples of problems:

Albemarle-Pamlico Sounds, N.C.	Wetlands loss; erosion; runoff
Barnegat Bay, N.J.	Nutrients; population growth; fisheries and species loss
Buzzards Bay, Mass.	Nutrients; pathogens; seafood contamination
Casco Bay, Maine	Toxins; fisheries loss; storm-water runoff
Charlotte Harbor, Fla.	Red/brown tides; population growth
Corpus Christi Bay, Texas	Population; pollution; harvest declines — oyster & white shrimp
Delaware Inland Bays, Del.	Nutrients; algal blooms; red/brown tides
Galveston Bay, Texas	Habitat loss; pollution
Indian River Lagoon, Fla.	Toxins; fisheries loss; population growth
Long Island Sound, N.Y., Conn.	Excessive nitrogen; low levels of oxygen
Maryland Coastal Bays, Md.	Nutrients; toxins; population growth
Mobile Bay, Ala.	Pathogens; runoff; population growth
Morro Bay, Calif.	Contaminated seafood; nutrients; pathogens
Narragansett Bay, R.I.	Habitat loss; fisheries loss; toxins
Peconic Bay, N.Y.	Fecal coliform; toxins; brown tides
Puget Sound, Wash.	Population growth; pathogens; habitat loss
San Francisco Bay, Calif.	Population; habitat loss
San Juan Bay, Puerto Rico	Pollution; species loss
Santa Monica Bay, Calif.	Nutrients; contaminated seafood
Tampa Bay, Fla.	Nutrients; habitat loss

SOURCES: U.S. Environmental Protection Agency, Office of Water, National Estuary Program

treatment, and agricultural fertilizers and nutrients have polluted coastal waters, threatened spawning grounds, and added to the problem of back-bay flooding.

"I think the oceans and bays are trying to tell us something," says Fred McManus, a U.S. Environmental Protection Agency scientist in Atlanta. "When you see algal blooms, red tides, brown tides, pfiesteria in the Albemarle-Pamlico Sounds and Chesapeake Bay, manatees dying on the west coast of Florida, problems with coral reefs, problems with estuaries, we're not doing something right."

In some cases, regulators appear almost to be throwing up their hands at the challenges.

"When I hired on I expected to work with a law that protects wetlands. I soon found out the basic intent was to issue building permits," said Ernie Jahnke of the U.S. Army Corps of Engineers' Wilmington, N.C. office. "Some permits are denied. Most are issued — issued at best with modest review."

Environmentalists and government officials say the bays can be restored — at a hefty cost to taxpayers. Federal programs are proliferating; by one count, there are more than 70. But the subsidies are helping to underwrite a new wave of development, and exacerbating environmental pressures.

"What happens is, we solve one problem and end up causing another," says Scott W. Nixon, a coastal pollution expert at the University of Rhode Island. "You put in sewers and that improves water quality but also attracts more development, which means more people and the pollution problems that come with more people."

Some of the challenges confronting back-bay areas include:

Effects of development. Nationally, back bays are suffering from pollution such as toxic contaminants, loss of critical wildlife habitats, beach closures, overfishing, and harmful algal blooms — all associated with development. In New Jersey, a network of 7,133 pipes and ditches carries degraded storm water, often containing fecal bacteria, into the back bays. The state has a list of the pipes but does not require permits for the discharges. "There is no enforcement in this program," said David McPartland, a Department of Environmental Protection official.

Flood risks. The building boom along the back bays coincides with rising water levels, eroding shorelines, and increased runoff from storms — a sure formula for costly flood damage. An analysis of 1990s flood claims shows that New Jersey's back-bay communities account for a larger share of losses than its oceanfront resorts. Nationally, owners are responding by erecting seawalls and bulkheads, which harm nesting grounds for birds and sea turtles and close off public access to bays and beaches.

A myriad of federal programs, with an annual budget topping $1 billion, has been created to help manage and restore fragile back bays. The programs range from collecting untreated waste from weekend boaters to controlling storm-water runoff. Proponents says these programs have helped reduce pollution. But the growing list of taxpayer-funded programs highlights another political reality: The high cost of accommodating development in vulnerable coastal areas.

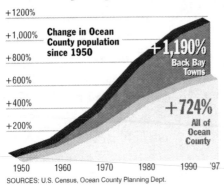

Back Bay Population Boom

Change in Ocean County population since 1950

+1,190% Back Bay Towns

+724% All of Ocean County

SOURCES: U.S. Census, Ocean County Planning Dept.

The chase for tax dollars. Property taxes are increasing rapidly as back-bay communities struggle to keep up with unprecedented growth. That's because the cost of accommodating new houses — water lines and sewers, roads, police, fire services, garbage collection, new schools — is greater than what each new house generates in taxes. This has spawned a futile chase for tax ratables, as communities approve more development in search of revenues to cover their costs. "Officials are doing the math. They know they have to slow down the growth," said Judy Jengo, deputy commissioner of the New Jersey Department of Environmental Protection.

A 1993 proposal to steer future growth into areas that are already developed should help, Jengo said, but seven years later, developers and environmentalists are still fighting over the details.

"The barrier islands are already built out, so we can't have much impact there. But we think the rule will do a much better job of containing the sprawl you're seeing," Jengo said.

If so, the changes can't come soon enough, environmentalists say.

Barnegat Bay, a 40-mile-long estuary stretching from Bay Head to Stafford Township, faces unprecedented development pressures. Bordered by lush sea meadows, tidal pools and salt marshes, the bay serves as a marine breeding ground and is an important stopover for migrating birds. But because of its shallow depth and poor drainage, it is especially vulnerable to pollution.

A 1993 state study reported that the Barnegat Bay watershed was one of the fastest-growing areas in the state. Population had quadrupled since 1950, to 435,000, with the figure swelling even higher in summer months. All of the people, cars, boats and development were harming water quality, the report concluded.

Since then, pressures have only intensified, scientists and planners say, as a booming economy has spawned a new wave of building. Richard Lathrop, a Rutgers University scientist, estimates that 70 percent of the Barnegat Bay shoreline — an area within 150 feet of the bay or its fringing salt marshes — is developed.

Nearly two-thirds of Ocean County's rapidly expanding population — or 288,000 people — live in the towns fringing the bay. New developments are sprouting almost weekly around the central and southern portions of the bay. And proposals that would add thousands more houses are under consideration.

"For years, the back-bay area was seen as a backward, sort of piney, out-of-the-way place where people didn't want to live," said Andy Strauss, a former adviser to Gov. Thomas Kean on development issues. "Now ... you're seeing central and southern Ocean County mushroom. Unfortunately, state planning programs don't really address the critical growth-management issues."

The Department of Environmental Protection has been tracking the health of Barnegat Bay for decades. Its studies have consistently found that water quality is being hurt by increased development. But efforts to control building along back bays have had a limited effect at best.

"I have more questions than answers about the environmental quality of Barnegat Bay," said Michael Kennish of Rutgers' Institute of Marine and Coastal Sciences. "There is no question development is having an effect on water quality. The biggest problem is runoff from roofs and lawns. But you also have problems with metals and oil pollution and boats. On some days, it's so crowded you can practically walk across the bay on the boats."

An estimated 50,000 boats use the bay each year — or about 40 percent of all boats in the state.

Some use the bay as their toilet. "After some weekends, I'll find toilet paper and human feces in the eelgrass three miles up the bay from where the boats park. It smells like a toilet out there," said Pete McLain, a former state environmental official, who is working to clean up the bay. "If a small town dumped all of its crap in the street, you'd hear about it."

In 1995, Congress added Barnegat Bay to the Environmental Protection Agency's National Estuaries Program, a plan that aims to protect 28 of the nation's most sensitive estuaries. Scientists and government officials are completing a study of the bay and drafting a management plan, which they hope to submit to federal regulators this year.

Some members contend that the Barnegat Bay program has struggled to define its mission and has shied away from the most important issue facing the bay — how to deal with rapid development. "It's a lot of fluff," said Spodofora. "I'm a member and I'm not even sure what they're doing."

"It's not an easy process," said Bob Scro, who took over the program last spring. "But the program has made some positive strides in the last year."

Scro points to the state's successful restoration of the Navesink River in northern New Jersey as a model for Barnegat Bay. "We have unrestricted shellfish harvesting there for the first time in 30 years."

A sewer line, then growth

Stafford Township, tucked between the Pinelands to the west and Barnegat Bay to the east, might seem an unlikely crossroads for the debate over coastal sprawl. For most of its history, the area was little more than a place to gas up and buy a bag of ice on the way to Long Beach Island. And that suited the locals just fine.

Many lived off the water, harvesting oysters, clams and crabs, which they sold to restaurants. The vast expanse of bay, with its golden sea meadows and lush marshes, defined their identities and the geography of the place, too.

"There was hardly any growth. We had so much open space, no one was really concerned about development," Spodofora said. The 53-year-old engineer grew up here.

His children attended the same small elementary school that he had. "It was a quiet little place, which is why I stayed."

Martha Kremer, the township zoning officer, recalls that in the 1960s a developer put up a billboard on Route 72 advertising lots for a new development: Ocean Acres. For years, lots sold slowly. Then, in 1989, the township used state funds to run a sewer line to the development, which abuts the Pinelands. "And all hell broke loose," Kremer said. "Everybody wanted to build."

Kremer delivers this historical note as she and Spodofora pause to inspect the latest row of new homes being carved out of uplands on the western fringe of the township. There are now nearly 3,700 houses in Ocean Acres, and bigger, more expensive homes are going up daily. The tract, which is spread over nearly 80 acres, accounts for one-third of the nearly 10,700 homes in the township.

When built out, Ocean Acres is expected to have 5,309 homes — a 43 percent increase from today. The township's population is expected to climb from about 19,000 today to 39,000. That would be a nearly 11-fold increase from 1970. The population grew by 40 percent between 1990 and 1996 alone.

Property values are rising so quickly that the township has conducted three reassessments since 1984. That year, officials estimated that property was worth $200 million. It is now worth $1.4 billion, and climbing. Lots that sold for $10,000 as recently as two years ago now fetch $30,000 to $40,000.

"We're seeing change in the township on almost a daily basis," Spodofora said.

Where are all the people coming from? A popular misconception, Kremer says, is that they are retirees. Only one in five residents is over 65. Many have moved from the crowded suburbs of North Jersey and Philadelphia. A surprising number still commute up the Garden State Parkway to their old jobs. "You see the cars leaving at 6 a.m.," Kremer said. Nearly half live along the lagoons and waterways of the bay.

Spodofora calculates that it costs the township $1.17 in services for each $1 in taxes it collects on a single-family home. The tax bill on a home assessed at the township average of $114,000 is about $2,600.

The township has the advantage of a healthy commercial tax base along the south side of Route 72, a major highway. That helps to offset what it loses on residential property. And new commercial proposals keep arriving. The township also is bordered by several large, government-owned tracts, including the Forsythe National Wildlife Refuge. "Having open spaces helps keep your taxes down," Spodofora said.

The school district, Southern Regional, is heavily subsidized by wealthy property owners on nearby Long Beach Island. This is an artifact of the island's extraordinary real estate values and the state's reliance on property taxes to fund schools. Most of the more than 15,000 properties on the island are vacation homes. And about 85 percent of the island's owners live elsewhere during the school year. Yet their property taxes still go to Southern Regional. The six resort towns on Long Beach Island account for about 13 percent of the students at Southern Regional, but provide 75 percent of the district's $18.2 million budget. That works out to an average cost of $36,325 for each of the 365 island students — or more than the cost of a year at Harvard.

Stafford Township represents 45 percent (1,345) of the

students but only 25 percent of the budget.

"It's definitely odd," Spodofora said. "But I am thankful."

The American Dream

A 1979 state report found that at least 10,000 acres of salt marsh had been dredged and filled to create lagoon developments along the bays between Sandy Hook and Cape May before a state law halted the practice. Developers carved the canals and placed the dredged material on peninsulas between the canals, elevating the land high enough to build.

As many as 30,000 lots were created this way in the 1950s and 1960s, often with the help of the state, which sold developers its title to the land underneath the water.

The practice obliterated estuarine habitats that had served as vital spawning grounds for fish and crabs and shellfish. Developers had a different view. They were helping to build the future, provide jobs, and create the American Dream.

"We sold to people who never dreamed they could own a second home: clerks, cops, garbage men, nurses. You could buy a modest house, including a waterfront, for $290 down and a $6,700 mortgage," said Herbert Shapiro. Along with his late brother, Shapiro built approximately 3,500 houses in the Beach Haven West section of Stafford Township. "Then the state came along and said, 'You're ruining the environment.' "

Spodofora says the lagoons are an environmental sore spot in the township. "Lagoons have an inability to flush properly," he says. "The problem is you get stagnant water with contaminants. Some of those contaminants from runoff make it into the bay. We're now dealing with the sins of the past."

The township and Spodofora have won praise for their efforts to control storm-water runoff, pollution, and back-bay flooding. They have reconfigured storm drains and building codes so rainwater recharges into the earth, instead of running down paved streets and pipes into the bay. Spodofora has enlisted residents to monitor drains, tagging and numbering each one, so they can call him when they clog.

In the 1980s, township officials, recognizing that development was imminent, rewrote their master plan. They increased lot sizes in sensitive areas to discourage building. Last year, they helped persuade residents to back a countywide open-space proposal, costing 1.2 cents per $100 of assessed value. The funds will be used to acquire undeveloped tracts throughout Ocean County.

Stafford Township is now considered a model for other back-bay towns. "I wish all of the municipal officials were as enlightened as John Spodofora," said deCamp, whose group has battled many back-bay communities over building plans.

"I know as an engineer you don't know if something actually works until it's tested," Spodofora says. "Sometimes the real world surprises you."

The rising level of back bays is one such example.

"A lot of people when they think of sea-level rise think only of the ocean," said James G. Titus, an Environmental Protection Agency scientist who has written extensively about rising sea levels. He points out that bays have risen at about the same rate as oceans — approximately 16 inches in the last 100 years in New Jersey.

Even tiny rises can result in significant increases in

flood damage, erosion of bay-front beaches, and a costly rush to rescue property owners.

"The bay shoreline is being drowned," said Norbert P. Psuty, a Rutgers University geologist, "and flooding is more frequent."

During hurricanes and nor'easters, water piles into the back bays and sounds and has nowhere to go. Depending on the wind direction, it may get pushed over low-lying developments rimming the bay, or flood the backsides of the barrier islands, as it did in September during Hurricane Floyd.

"Our worst flooding was on the sound side," said Bruce M. Bortz, town planner for Nags Head, N.C. Water from the Albemarle Sound was deep enough to float a flat-bottom skiff in some areas.

Where the Toms River empties into Barnegat Bay, Pine Beach Mayor Russell K. Corby said flooding had worsened. He estimated the small town had lost 10 to 20 percent of its beaches to flood-related erosion since 1991. "We have a whole group of towns going through the same thing," Corby said. "But it doesn't get the same attention as ocean towns."

Back-bay towns also took the brunt of a powerful nor'easter that pushed unrivaled floodwaters into Barnegat Bay in December 1992.

An analysis of disaster loans found that businesses and homeowners in back-bay towns collected nearly $18 million in subsidized Small Business Administration loans, while ocean resorts received $15 million. Stafford Township was awarded more loans than Atlantic City, Ocean City, Cape May or Stone Harbor.

Leona C. Zarharchuck was finishing repairs from another flood when the 1992 storm pushed 39 inches of mud and water into her home on Mallard Drive in Stafford Township. "I had just put new carpet down," she said.

Zarharchuck lives along a tidal creek that empties into Barnegat Bay. Nor'easters routinely push bay water up the creek. "I have had three floods since I moved here" in 1976, Zarharchuck said. "When bay water meets the creek, it's over."

Zarharchuck took out a $10,000 SBA loan to elevate her house. She collected $18,000 in federally backed flood insurance from another storm.

"What I think is happening," she said, "is the ground is lowering and the water is getting higher."

Pollution comes with sprawl

BERKELEY TOWNSHIP, N.J. — Chris Smith and David Friedland are poking holes in the perfectly manicured lawn of Constantine Afansief's home 10 miles west of Barnegat Bay, in Ocean County.

Row upon row of compact new homes line the street. Each was carved out of uplands once thick with pine trees and hardwoods. After the trees were ripped out, the topsoil was scraped and covered with sod.

To the untrained eye, the lawn appears perfect. Yet when Smith tries to force a slim metal rod into the grass, to measure its ability to drain, the rod resists after an inch or two.

"The soil is really compact here," says Smith, a soil scientist with the U.S. Department of Agriculture. "This is pretty bad."

Afansief nods. "I tried to put in some plants ... but I couldn't get down deep enough."

Now rainwater is not able to soak into the earth.

Instead, Smith explains, it spills into the street, carrying lawn fertilizers with it. The nitrogen and phosphates become part of a chemical cocktail that eventually finds its way into the bay.

Scientists call this nonpoint pollution, a fancy term for pollution that accompanies sprawl. It is now far and away the biggest threat to Barnegat Bay and dozens of other estuaries.

"It's the pollution you get from too many people wanting to be in the same place," says Michael Kennish, a Rutgers University marine scientist.

In the 1950s and 1960s, the biggest environmental threats to Barnegat Bay were from sewage and industrial discharges. Regulators thought they solved those problems with stricter laws and by funding regional sewer systems. Water quality did improve. But the sewers unleashed a wave of development along back bays, with the population doubling in two decades.

The additional pollution from development, cars, pets, and increased boat traffic began to affect the bay. Excess nitrogen and phosphates accumulated. Algal blooms formed. The water became murky. Oxygen was depleted. Fecal bacteria counts rose. Beach closures increased.

"When you take these soils that are well-drained and you change the cover, you change the dynamics of the way water flows," says Friedland, director of the Ocean County Soil Conservation District. "People don't understand what they do here has an impact out there. We're trying to change that."

Pete McLain understands. He has spent countless hours on Barnegat Bay studying changes in the marine life and water quality.

"It's surprising what's in the water," he says. "A little bit of fertilizer is a good thing, but when you dump a ton on your lawn and it ends up in the bay, you create a problem. The water gets covered by phytoplankton. No light gets through to the grasses and they die. That's what nonpoint pollution does to the bay."

For 50 years, the craggy and blunt McLain worked as a wildlife biologist, serving part of that time as deputy director of the Division of Fish and Game. Now retired, he writes articles, operates an environmental center on Island Beach Park, and spends countless hours on the bay surveying eelgrass.

"Eelgrass is the biological backbone of the bay," he shouts, as he angles his battered Boston Whaler through the chop and spray toward a sedge island near Barnegat Lighthouse. "If you take it away, you won't have the crabs. Clams, crabs, fish — all are supported by it."

As the clear August light plays off the eelgrass, all seems well until McLain runs his rake across the bottom of a shallow pool of water. Most of the grass he hauls up is withered and brown. The few fresh strands are short. "By this time of the year, they should be twice as long," he says.

"People say the bay is healthy, but it's not," McLain shouts as the boat bounces back across the water. "You've got every beach town around here producing pollution. Whenever it rains, all of the oil and garbage and even the dog poop washes into the water."

One of the most troublesome spots is Tice's Shoals, off the southern tip of Island Beach State Park. As many as 500 sailboats and pleasure craft anchor here on weekends. Some owners use the bay as a toilet.

In 1992, Congress passed the Federal Clean Vessel Act, paying 75 percent of the cost of new pumpout boats and marina outlets with funds from a tax on motor fuel. Since then, the program has spent $19.5 million to install nearly 3,000 pumpout stations, including 152 in New Jersey.

McLain, who helped to get a pumpout boat for Barnegat Bay, says it has helped reduce pollution.

"It's doing a great job," he says. "Everybody loves it because there's no charge and it's convenient. Convenience is the word."

Nature retains control

ISLAND BEACH STATE PARK, N.J. — Bill Vibbert eases down on the gas pedal of his salt-stained jeep and the rattling engine starts to pull ahead. The vehicle climbs to 36 m.p.h., still not fast enough to overtake the sharp-shinned hawk the park superintendent is chasing.

"That hawk is doing at least 40 m.p.h. into a pretty stiff southwest wind," Vibbert says, watching the bird glide over a deep thicket toward Barnegat Bay. "That is something you just don't see every day."

Not along the most densely built shoreline in America, anyway. But on Island Beach, a 9.5-mile oasis of rolling dunes, freshwater ponds, and shaded maritime forest, it's not rare. The October skies are scribbled with hawks, migrating songbirds, ospreys and mallards. During storms, black ducks pile into Spizzle Creek, a protected tidal marsh. "There used to be so many, you would see black clouds out over the bay," Vibbert says.

The energetic park superintendent has run Island Beach for a decade and is well aware of its special role as one of the last unspoiled stretches along the New Jersey coast. Just beyond the park entrance, row after row of cottages crowd the beach. Farther north, boardwalks, condominiums and motels line the highway. And to the south,

JOHN COSTELLO / Inquirer Staff Photographer
Tightly packed homes of South Seaside Park yield to the sanctuary of Island Beach State Park.

across Barnegat Inlet, lies Long Beach Island with its lavish beachfront homes renting for thousands of dollars a week.

"This is precious real estate," Vibbert says. "It is amazing it is still in this virgin state."

In 1933, when Island Beach was in private hands, the owners sold a limited number of passes to fishermen, hikers and bathers. The rules were simple: "Leave things be. Don't trample the sand dunes. Don't pick the flowers, and don't annoy the osprey."

Seven decades later, Vibbert's job is to ensure that Island Beach remains a pristine sanctuary.

Last year, one million visitors entered Island Beach. Most came by car during the peak summer season. Some biked in. Others parked their boats and waded ashore.

The sanctuary has limited parking space by design. The main road, a two-lane blacktop, stops more than a mile from the south end of the island.

As a barrier island, the beach is constantly changing, adding sand here and losing sand there. But unlike in most New Jersey shore towns, the park staff does not attempt to control nature. There are no rock walls, groins, or seawalls on the beach. And the park has never received beachfill, Vibbert says.

"I don't think we're very high on the list in terms of protecting property and investments," the superintendent says. Not that he is complaining. "If you design a beach, this is how you would want it to look."

In the 1800s, wealthy industrialists traveled by train from Philadelphia and New York to use the hunting and fishing clubs. Later, Babe Ruth and Woodrow Wilson vacationed here.

Henry Phipps, a Philadelphian who made his fortune as Andrew Carnegie's partner in Pittsburgh Steel, bought the island in 1926 with plans to develop it into an exclusive seaside resort. But those plans collapsed with the stock market in 1929 and were not revived for decades.

In the 1950s, Phipps' heirs attempted to sell the island to Massachusetts developers for more than $3 million. A private group that included former President Herbert Hoover and Richard H. Pough, an executive at the American Museum of Natural History, made a counteroffer. Then fate interceded.

Pough's museum held garden parties for its benefactors. One of the regulars at those affairs was the mother of New Jersey Gov. Alfred E. Driscoll. "She was sort of indoctrinated on this, and sort of twisted her son's arm," Pough recalled. Driscoll persuaded the legislature to use $2.7 million to set the island aside as a state park.

"Isn't that amazing? You think of all the people who have enjoyed this park over the years and it all goes back to Dick Pough meeting with the governor's mother," Vibbert says.

The 3,000 acres of park are a rich mixture of windswept dunes covered with sedge grass and seaside goldenrod that attracts migrating monarch butterflies. Dense inland pockets of bayberry, beach heather and Virginia creeper border salt marshes, cranberry bogs and freshwater ponds that formed when the 1962 Ash Wednesday Storm breached the island.

Vibbert relies heavily on volunteers and grants to make improvements, adding accessible trails for the disabled and a new nature center.

"We recognize this is a government operation and we face certain restraints," he says.

"I love this park," Vibbert adds. "When I have a day off, I don't go anywhere. I visit Island Beach."

ELIZABETH V. ROBERTSON / Inquirer Suburban Staff
People say the bay is healthy, but it's not," says Pete McLain, a retired wildlife biologist and former New Jersey environmental official.

About the Authors

Tony Wood has been a reporter and editor more than 25 years, including 19 at The Inquirer. Wood is the paper's resident expert on weather and climate issues, about which he has written extensively. He has reported about nor'easters in New Jersey, hurricanes in North Carolina and tornadoes in Florida. Wood attended Temple University and was a National Endowment for the Humanities Fellow at the University of Michigan, where he studied Latin American politics, along with meteorology.

Gil Gaul has been a reporter and editor 25 years, the last 17 at the Inquirer. He has written about topics ranging from organized crime to the growth of nonprofits to libraries to the safety of the nation's blood supply. He is a two-time winner of the Pulitzer Prize. Gaul is a graduate of Fairleigh Dickinson University and was a Nieman Fellow at Harvard University, studying business, health and law.

The Inquirer stories were edited by David Zucchino and copy edited by Emmet Linn. John Costello and Elizabeth V. Roberston took most of the photographs. Matthew Ericson produced the graphics and designed this book.